Japanese Folktales and Legends

An Enthralling Collection of Stories, Mythical Creatures, Heroes, and Timeless Tales

Free limited time bonus

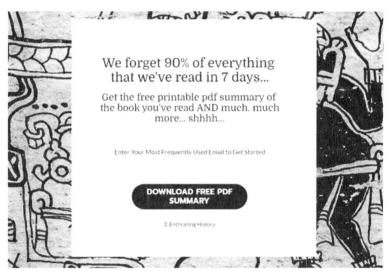

Stop for a moment. We have a free bonus set up for you. The problem is this: we forget 90% of everything that we read after 7 days. Crazy fact, right? Here's the solution: we've created a printable, 1-page pdf summary for this book that you're reading now. All you have to do to get your free pdf summary is to go to the following website: **https://livetolearn.lpages.co/enthrallinghistory/**

Or, Scan the QR code!

Once you do, it will be intuitive. Enjoy, and thank you!

Table of Contents

Introduction

In every corner of the world, folktales and legends have been an essential part of cultures, passed down through generations as sources of wisdom, caution, and inspiration. The history of these stories is as old as humanity itself, originating from the earliest times when people sought to explain the mysteries of the natural world, teach moral lessons, and preserve their cultural heritage.

The journey through the history of folktales and legends reveals how societies have understood and interacted with their world. From tales of the mythological gods of Greece to the trickster spirits of African folklore, these stories have shaped human history and culture, serving as mirrors that reflect the hopes, fears, and aspirations of their storytellers.

In Japan, folktales and legends hold a special place in the nation's cultural heritage. These stories are not merely entertainment; they offer insights into the Japanese way of life, values, and deep connection with nature. Two of the most significant historical texts that capture these ancient stories are the *Nihon Shoki* and the *Kojiki*.

The *Nihon Shoki*, also known as *The Chronicles of Japan*, is one of the oldest histories of Japan, completed in 720 AD. It was commissioned by the imperial court and offers a comprehensive account of Japan's early history, from the creation of the world to the eighth century. The *Nihon Shoki* is written in classical Chinese and is considered a fundamental text for understanding Japan's early myths, including the tales of the kami, or gods, and the legendary emperors.

The *Kojiki*, or *Records of Ancient Matters*, predates the *Nihon Shoki* and was completed in 712 AD. Unlike the *Nihon Shoki*, the *Kojiki* is written in a mixture of classical Chinese and phonetic Japanese. It provides a more intimate and poetic account of Japan's creation myths, the genealogy of the gods, and the deeds of early emperors. The *Kojiki* is treasured for its vivid storytelling and its preservation of the earliest forms of Japanese language and myth.

These two texts are not just historical records; they are the foundation of Japan's mythological heritage. They offer a window into the ancient world of the Japanese people, where gods walked the earth and the natural world was imbued with divine presence. Through these chronicles, the creation of the Japanese islands by the divine couple Izanagi and Izanami, the exploits of the sun goddess Amaterasu, and the heroic deeds of legendary warriors are revealed.

Apart from these ancient texts focusing on myths, many written records detail stories and folktales that carry the wisdom of the elders. These stories have been passed down through generations, capturing the essence of Japanese culture and the collective wisdom of its people. Tales of cunning animals, wise elders, and brave heroes provide moral lessons and reflect the values and beliefs that have shaped Japanese society.

As our exploration into the folktales and legends of Japan begins, we enter a realm where the lines between the natural and the supernatural blur. These stories are populated with powerful deities, brave samurai, cunning tricksters, and fearsome yokai (supernatural creatures). However, the myths and legends explored in this book are more than just stories; they are living traditions that continue to influence contemporary Japanese culture.

Chapter 1 – Tales from Ancient Times

In ancient Japan, nestled between lush forests and sparkling rivers, there lay a small village. The thatched-roof houses, built from wood and straw, clustered together. Smoke curled lazily from the chimneys, mingling with the morning mist that hung low over the fields. The scent of fresh rice, harvested from the terraced paddies that hugged the hillsides, filled the air, mixing with the earthy aroma of the surrounding woods.

Children ran barefoot through the narrow dirt paths, their laughter echoing. The villagers went about their daily tasks with a sense of purpose. Farmers tended to their crops, fishermen cast their nets into the crystal-clear streams, and artisans crafted tools and pottery with practiced hands. Life here moved in rhythm with the seasons.

Beyond this serene village, the land of Japan stretched out in all directions, a mosaic of mountains, rivers, and forests. Majestic volcanoes pierced the horizon, their peaks shrouded in swirling mists, standing like silent sentinels watching over the archipelago. It was a land where the very ground seemed alive, where mountains whispered secrets to the wind and rivers sang ancient songs as they wound their way to the sea. Ancient forests, dense and teeming with life, cloaked the landscape, their leaves rustling like the soft murmur of a thousand voices. The air was thick with the scent of blooming flowers and fertile soil.

Mount Yōtei, an active stratovolcano in Hokkaido.[1]

This, however, was not always the case: scientists believe that the Japanese islands were under the sea before the Miocene. From a scientific perspective, this enchanting archipelago was born from the clashing of tectonic plates. For millions of years, the relentless forces of the Earth's crust had been at work beneath the ocean, pushing and pulling, creating massive earthquakes and volcanic eruptions. The Pacific Plate and the Philippine Sea Plate collided and subducted, forcing the seafloor to buckle and fold, giving birth to underwater mountains that eventually breached the surface. These geological processes sculpted the islands, resulting in towering peaks and expansive valleys.

However, there was another explanation for the creation of this land. The people of ancient Japan saw their world as not just the result of natural forces but as a place imbued with spirit and magic. To them, the mountains, rivers, and forests were not mere geographical features but living entities, each with its own soul and story. The volcanoes were the abodes of fiery deities, and the forests were sanctuaries for countless spirits.

The Legend of Izanagi and Izanami, the Two Creators of Japan

One such legend that talks about the birth of the Japanese islands begins with two divine figures: Izanagi and Izanami. It all started when these celestial beings stood on the stairway of heaven known as Ama-no-hashidate. Here, they gazed upon the chaotic expanse below, seeing nothing but a vast, dark, and lifeless ocean. In their hands they held a jeweled spear. They dipped the spear into the primordial waters, stirring the chaos. When they lifted the spear back out, droplets of water fell into the ocean, solidifying into land. The very first island, Onogoro-shima, had been created.

It was on this sacred island that Izanagi and Izanami decided to make their new home. They built a palace and prepared for their wedding ceremony. Central to their new abode was a majestic pillar (or another spear, according to other sources). Around this pillar, the two gods performed a ritual to consecrate their union. Izanagi and Izanami circled the pillar in opposite directions. However, as they passed each other, Izanami spoke first, breaking the sacred order.

Izanagi and Izanami, stirring the ocean with the legendary spear to create Japan.[2]

The consequences of this mistake were immediate and profound, yet they did not directly affect the two gods. Instead, the consequences fell onto their first child. Known as Hiruko, the child was born without bones. Disheartened, they placed Hiruko in a basket and set him adrift on the sea, hoping the waters might show him mercy. Despite his tragic beginning, Hiruko would later become known as Ebisu, the patron of fishermen and one of the seven gods of good luck. He was revered for his resilience.

Undeterred, Izanagi and Izanami continued their efforts, giving birth next to the island of Awa. Yet, they were not satisfied with the result. Confused, they turned to the seven invisible gods, their parents, who revealed the reason behind their misfortunes. The gods explained that their improper performance of the marriage ritual had caused their misfortune. Determined to set things right, Izanagi and Izanami repeated the ceremony, this time ensuring that Izanagi spoke first.

With the ritual properly completed, their union flourished. Together, they created the eight principal islands of Japan: Awaji, Shikoku, Oki, Tsukushi (Kyushu), Iki, Tsushima, Sado, and Oyamato. These islands became the heart of the Japanese archipelago. But the islands were not their only progeny. Izanagi and Izanami also gave birth to a multitude of divine beings, known as kami.

A map showing Japan's major cities and islands.[3]

The concept of kami is deeply rooted in the essence of Japanese spirituality. Kami are not just gods but also spirits that inhabit all things, both animate and inanimate. They can be the spirits of nature, ancestors, or even ideas and forces. Among the notable children of Izanagi and Izanami were Oho-wata-tsu-mi, the god of the sea; Kuku-no-shi, the god of trees; and Oho-yama-tsu-mi, the god of mountains.

These kami embodied the natural elements and forces that shaped the world. They were revered and worshiped, and their presence was felt in every corner of the land. But luck was not meant to linger around the divine couple for long. Izanami was destined to face her demise the moment she gave birth to another kami known as Kagutsuchi, the god of fire.

The birth of Kagutsuchi was a scene of both wonder and tragedy. As Izanami labored, the very air seemed to crackle with intensity. The process was excruciatingly painful, and Izanami's screams and cries filled the heavens. Her tears transformed into many more kami. Despite Izanami's agony, Kagutsuchi was successfully brought into the world, blazing with the fierce energy of a newborn god of fire. But Izanami's injuries were grievous, and she succumbed to the fatal burns inflicted during the birth.

Izanagi's reaction to his celestial wife's death was one of overwhelming rage and despair. Enraged, he unsheathed his sword and, with swift vengeance, sliced Kagutsuchi into pieces. From each fragment of the god of fire, more kami sprang forth, their forms emerging from the smoldering remains. However, Izanagi's fury quickly turned into great sadness. Unable to bear the loss of his beloved Izanami, he resolved to follow her into the underworld, known in the Japanese tongue as Yomi.

In the gloomy and foreboding realm of Yomi, Izanagi sought out Izanami, determined to bring her back. But he was too late; Izanami had already consumed food in the underworld, binding her to that desolate place. Forbidden from returning to the realm of the living, Izanami listened to Izanagi's desperate pleas and agreed to negotiate with the gods of the underworld. However, before he left, she made him promise one thing: Izanagi must be patient and not attempt to see her while she sought a way to return to the land of the living.

Time passed, but to Izanagi, it passed at an excruciatingly slow pace. His heart undoubtedly ached with longing. Unable to wait any longer, he broke his promise and lit a torch to see his beloved wife, perhaps hoping a glance at her could cure his sadness. However, what he saw filled him with horror and sorrow. Izanami's once beautiful form was now a decomposing corpse, ravaged by death. The sight of her decayed body shattered Izanagi's heart.

Enraged by his betrayal, Izanami called upon the hags of hell to pursue the fleeing Izanagi. These demons, grotesque and relentless, chased after him with fervor. As Izanagi fled, he threw seeds behind him, which grew into grapevines and other plants, entangling the hags and slowing their pursuit. Desperate to escape, Izanagi also tossed peaches, known in ancient Japan for their mystical powers, to distract and fend off his pursuers.

Finally reaching the outside world, Izanagi quickly grasped a colossal boulder and hauled it to block the entrance to Yomi, sealing it before Izanami could reach him. This, however, did not stop Izanami from cursing her husband one last time. Through the barrier, their voices echoed in the dark, final confrontation. Enraged and heartbroken, Izanami not only cursed her once beloved husband, but also vowed to claim a thousand lives each day as retribution. In response, Izanagi, with a heavy heart, declared that he would ensure 1,500 new lives were born each day. This exchange symbolized the perpetual cycle of life and death.

Yomotsu Hirasaka, believed to be a border between Yomi and the world of the living.[4]

Having sealed the entrance to the underworld, Izanagi was determined to rid himself of the impurities he had accumulated during his journey through Yomi. He traveled to the river Woto, where he prepared to perform a cleansing ritual to purify his body and soul. Standing in the clear, flowing waters, Izanagi began to wash away the taint of the underworld.

As he washed his left eye, the brilliant sun goddess Amaterasu emerged, her radiance lighting up the heavens. Next, Izanagi cleansed his right eye, and from it came Tsuki-yomi, the god of the moon, whose serene light complemented his sister's brilliance. When Izanagi washed his nose, the storm god Susanoo was born, embodying the fierce and untamed power of nature. Additionally, the god of wind, Shina-tsu-hiko, emerged from Izanagi's breath. These deities would soon become the principal gods of Shinto, central to both spiritual and cultural aspects of Japan to this day.

But the birth of gods did not end there. As Izanagi cast off his clothes, twelve more deities sprang into existence, each piece of clothing giving life to a new divine being.

Shinto

Shinto is deeply rooted in the country's history, nature, and culture. Unlike many organized religions, Shinto does not have a founder, a sacred scripture, or a fixed set of doctrines. Instead, it revolves around the worship of kami, emphasizing the relationship between humans and nature.

Shinto, which means "the way of the gods," is an animistic belief system where every element of the natural world is considered sacred. The kami are seen as manifestations of the divine essence in all things, from towering mountains and ancient trees to rivers and stones. This belief fosters a profound respect for nature and an understanding of the interconnectedness of all life.

However, Shinto beliefs extend beyond the kami. They encompass many spirits and supernatural beings that inhabit the natural world, each with its own unique traits and stories.

One such tale is of the spirit known as Yuki-onna, who is both beautiful and deadly, embodying the dual nature of winter. Believed to dwell in the remote, snow-covered mountains of Japan, Yuki-onna is often described as a tall, ethereal figure with long, flowing hair as black as a winter's night and skin as pale as freshly fallen snow. Her eyes, cold and piercing, can enchant or terrify those who meet her gaze. She drifts silently through the blizzards, her white kimono blending seamlessly with the snowy landscape, making her appear almost ghostly.

Yuki-onna's story varies across different regions of Japan, but a common theme is her dual nature—capable of both kindness and cruelty. In some tales, she is a protective spirit who watches over travelers lost in the snow, guiding them to safety or providing a peaceful death for those who are beyond saving. In others, she is a vengeful spirit who preys on those who dare to invade her frozen domain, freezing them with her icy breath or leading them astray until they succumb to the cold.

A depiction of Yuki-onna, c. 1700.[5]

One of the most well-known versions of Yuki-onna's tale involves a young woodcutter named Minokichi and his mentor, Mosaku. One bitterly cold night, as a blizzard raged outside, Minokichi and Mosaku sought shelter in a small, abandoned hut. Exhausted, they fell into a deep sleep. In the middle of the night, Minokichi awoke to see a stunningly beautiful woman, dressed in white, standing over Mosaku. Her breath froze him to death.

Terrified, Minokichi lay still, watching the woman as she turned her gaze upon him. She approached, her cold breath chilling him to the bone. Just as she was about to freeze him, she paused, captivated by his youth and beauty. She told him that she would spare his life on the condition that he never speak of what he had seen. If he broke this promise, she would return and take his life.

Years passed, and Minokichi kept his promise, never speaking of that fateful night. He eventually met and married a beautiful woman named Oyuki, who appeared mysteriously one winter day. They lived happily together and had children, but somehow, Minokichi always felt a chill in Oyuki's presence. One night, unable to contain his secret any longer, he told Oyuki about his encounter with Yuki-onna.

As he finished his story, Oyuki's expression changed, and the warmth drained from her face. She revealed herself to be Yuki-onna, the very spirit who had spared his life years before. Angry, she shouted at Minokichi, reminding him of her promise to take his life should he ever tell the story of that fateful night. However, despite her sorrow and anger, she could not bring herself to kill him in front of their children. With tears of ice, she disappeared into the night, but not before warning Minokichi one last time, "Take care of our children or I will come after you. Without hesitation next time."

From then on, Minokichi never saw his wife again.

This tale of Yuki-onna shows the delicate balance between humans and nature in Shinto belief. It highlights the respect and reverence that must be shown to the spirits inhabiting the natural world, as well as the consequences of failing to honor these ancient bonds.

Shinto rituals and festivals, or matsuri, are vital aspects of Japanese culture, serving to honor the kami and maintain harmony with nature. Worship in Shinto is different from many other religions, focusing on rituals and offerings rather than prayer. The practice of purification, for one, is central to Shinto. Known as harae, this cleansing ritual was first performed by Izanagi upon his return from Yomi.

Harae is a fundamental practice in Shinto aimed at removing spiritual pollution, known as tsumi or kegare. Kegare encompasses impurities like death, disease, filth, and blood, while tsumi refers to wrongful actions such as crime, murder, or disrespecting elders.

Shinto does not preach an extensive set of ethics; neither does it promise a reward-based heaven or a punishment-based hell. Instead, it views nature as inherently good. Impurity is an anomaly that can be corrected or purified. For example, before interacting with a kami in rituals or prayer, it is essential to remove impurities to ensure harmony and respect. Almost all Shinto shrines feature water basins with wooden ladles for a purification ritual known as temizu. This practice involves washing first the left hand, then the right, and finally pouring water into the hands to rinse the mouth, symbolizing both internal and external purification.

Two Japanese women performing temizu.[6]

Another form of harae is misogi, which involves immersing oneself in natural bodies of water, such as the ocean or a waterfall, to cleanse and purify. Shubatsu, a purification practice using salt, is commonly observed at the beginning of a sumo match when salt is spread around the ring to ward off impurities. Additionally, there is a purification ritual involving a wand, known as the haraigushi, which is waved over a person, object, or plot of land. This ritual is often performed before construction work begins to purify the site and ensure it brings nothing but good fortune.

Shinto festivals, such as the New Year's celebration (Shogatsu), the Doll Festival (Hinamatsuri), and the Gion Matsuri in Kyoto, are occasions to honor the kami with offerings, dances, and prayers.

Shrines, the sacred spaces of Shinto, are places where the kami are enshrined and worshiped. Each shrine is dedicated to specific kami, and people visit to make offerings, participate in rituals, and seek blessings. The architecture of the shrines reflects the harmonious relationship between humans and nature, with torii gates marking the transition from the mundane to the sacred.

A torii gate.[7]

Shinto, with its deep reverence for nature and the kami, provides a unique perspective on spirituality. It emphasizes purity, respect for the natural world, and the importance of rituals in maintaining harmony. The practices and beliefs of Shinto continue to shape the cultural and spiritual landscape of Japan, reflecting a timeless connection to the divine forces that inhabit the world.

Chapter 2 – Tales of the Kami

The term kami is often translated as "god" or "deity." However, these translations do not fully capture the essence of what kami truly represents. As we discussed in the previous chapter, kami in Shinto can embody a wide range of entities. Kami can be god-like figures, such as Amaterasu, the sun goddess, or Hachiman, the god of war, or natural phenomena like mountains, rain, earthquakes, and storms. Even a solitary tree can embody the spirit of a kami, symbolizing the deep connection between nature and the divine in Japanese spirituality. To put it simply, anything in this world that evokes a sense of wonder or awe can be considered a kami.

One such example of this huge reverence for nature is the sacred camphor tree in Kayashima Station. This tree has stood for over seven centuries, witnessing the long history of Japan. The train station, on the other hand, was first opened in 1910 and was originally rather small and simple. Sixty years later, the region experienced rapid population growth. Overcrowding soon became a pressing issue, and plans for an expansion were put forward in the 1970s. Of course, these plans included the removal of the ancient camphor tree.

The decision to cut down the tree was not taken lightly. It quickly sparked a large uproar among the locals in the area. Stories soon began to circulate about the anger of a certain spirit residing in the tree and the various misfortunes that befell anyone who attempted to harm it. Legend has it that a worker who cut a branch of the ancient tree almost immediately developed a high fever. Another rumor spoke of a white snake, which the Japanese often consider an omen, wrapped around the tree. Others claimed they saw smoke rising from it, as if the tree was expressing its displeasure.

Kayashima Station today, with the sacred tree in the middle.[8]

Faced with these ominous signs and growing opposition from the community, station officials reconsidered their plans. Rather than removing the tree, they decided to incorporate it into the new station's design. Construction began in 1973 and was completed in 1980. Today, the camphor tree stands proudly in the middle of Kayashima Station. It even features a small shrine at its base, allowing commuters to offer their respects as they go about their daily lives.

The Kami of Hair

In the same spirit of reverence for nature and the divine, Shinto belief extends to even the most personal aspects of human life, such as hair. The kami associated with hair, known as Kamigami, is revered for its influence over this part of the human body. Interestingly, the only shrine dedicated to this unique kami is known as Mikami Jinja and can be found in Kyoto. At this shrine, people come to pray for various hair-related issues, particularly seeking help with baldness or other hair problems. It is believed that by honoring Kamigami, they can receive blessings that improve their hair's health and vitality.

However, unlike many other kami, the background of Kamigami is not so extensive. Kamigami is rooted in the life of a man named Masayuki Fujiwara, who lived many centuries ago. Renowned for his exceptional skills as a hairdresser, Masayuki gained fame for his ability to transform and enhance the beauty of his clients through his meticulous and artistic haircuts. His reputation spread far and wide, and he was celebrated not only for his technical skills but also for his understanding of the deeper significance of hair in Japanese culture.

After his death, Masayuki Fujiwara was venerated for his contributions to the art of hairdressing. His spirit was enshrined at Mikami Jinja, and he became the kami of hair.

The Kami of Rice

Rice has long held a place of immense importance in Japan, serving as both a staple food and a symbol of life and prosperity. From ancient times to the present day, rice cultivation has been central to Japanese society and culture. The history of rice in Japan dates back thousands of years, with evidence of its cultivation appearing around 300 BC. Rice was not just a dietary staple but also a measure of wealth and a form of currency, influencing the social and economic structures of early Japan.

The kami of rice, Inari, emerged as one of the most revered deities in Japanese folklore. Inari's significance extends beyond agriculture. In earlier Japan, Inari was also the patron of swordsmiths and merchants. The origins of Inari's worship can be traced back to the founding of the shrine at Inari Mountain in 711 AD, though some scholars suggest that the veneration of Inari began as early as the late fifth century.

One of the enduring legends associated with Inari tells of a time of great famine when Inari descended from Heaven to aid the people of Japan. Riding on a white fox, Inari brought with her sheaves of cereal grains. As she arrived, the swamps and waterlogged lands of ancient Japan began to yield a new crop, which would eventually be known as rice. This miraculous intervention alleviated the famine and cemented Inari's status as a benefactor of the Japanese people.

Inari's depictions are as diverse as the beliefs of her followers. She is often portrayed in three main forms: a young female food goddess, an old man carrying sheaves of rice, and an androgynous bodhisattva in Japanese Buddhism. This flexibility in depiction makes Inari a deeply personal and accessible deity. Inari is also closely associated with foxes, or kitsune, which are considered her messengers. These magical foxes are believed to possess shape-shifting abilities and can appear in various forms, including dragons, snakes, and even giant spiders.

One intriguing tale tells of a wicked man who was taught a lesson by Inari through her transformation into a giant spider. This form was intended to instill fear and drive home the importance of humility and respect.

The symbols associated with Inari are varied, with the fox being the most prominent. Fox statues, often adorned with red yodarekake (votive bibs), are commonly found at Inari shrines, symbolizing the foxes' role as messengers. These statues typically come in pairs, representing male and female, and hold various symbolic items in their mouths or beneath their paws, such as jewels, keys, sheaves of rice, scrolls, or fox cubs.

A statue of kitsune wearing a red yodarekake.[9]

Inari shrines are distinctive, marked by the iconic red torii gates that signify the entrance to a sacred space. These torii, along with parts of the shrine buildings, are painted a bright red, a color associated with protection against illness and misfortune in Shinto.

The head shrine of Inari, known as Fushimi Inari Taisha, is in Fushimi, Kyoto. It is the largest and most important Inari shrine in Japan, boasting approximately 10,000 torii gates that lead up to the main shrine building on Inariyama. This path of gates, known as Senbon Torii, creates a mesmerizing tunnel of red that guides worshipers on a spiritual journey up the mountain.

The thousands of torii gates at Fushimi Inari Taisha.[10]

Inari is also revered in Japanese Buddhism, where she is often depicted as female or androgynous and referred to as Dakiniten. In this form, she is represented as a bodhisattva and rides upon a flying white fox. This blending of Shinto and Buddhist traditions highlights Inari's significant role in Japanese spiritual life.

Raijin, the Kami of Thunder

Raijin is a dualistic spirit, embodying both the destructive power of storms and the life-giving rain essential for agriculture. His duality is central to his nature. While his storms can wreak havoc, they also bring the rain that nourishes crops and sustains life. This complex character makes Raijin a significant and multifaceted figure in Japanese mythology.

The story of Raijin's birth begins with Izanami, the goddess who died and descended into Yomi, the underworld. When Izanagi, her husband, ventured into Yomi to bring her back, he witnessed a horrifying scene.

Izanami, now a decaying corpse, had given birth to eight thunder deities from different parts of her body. These eight thunder kami represented various types of thunder: Great-Thunder from her head, Fire-Thunder from her chest, Black-Thunder from her stomach, Blossoming-Thunder from her womb, Young-Thunder from her left hand, Earth-Thunder from her right hand, Rumbling-Thunder from her left foot, and Couchant-Thunder from her right foot. Together, these eight manifestations form Raijin, the god of thunder and storms. Izanami commanded Raijin to pursue Izanagi out of Yomi after he broke his promise not to look at her decaying form.

Raijin's appearance reflects his fearsome nature. In a country frequently beset by powerful storms, it is no wonder that Raijin is depicted as menacing. His gravity-defying and wild, spiky hair mirrors the chaos of a storm, while his fierce eyes and sharp teeth add to his intimidating presence. Often, Raijin is shown with three fingers on each hand, representing the past, present, and future. Unlike many other Japanese deities who are draped in flowing robes, Raijin is typically depicted bare-chested, emphasizing his power. His appearance is so formidable that those who are not familiar with Japanese myth have sometimes mistaken him for an oni, the fearsome ogres of Japanese folklore.

Raijin is also frequently depicted with a halo around his body, adorned with symbols from Taoism, Buddhism, and Shinto, indicating his wide-reaching influence across different spiritual traditions. This halo distinguishes him from other deities and highlights his unique role in Japanese mythology.

Folding screens featuring Raijin (left) and the god of wind, Fujin (right).[11]

Raijin is often shown wielding hammers and drums, instruments with which he creates thunder. His companion is usually Fujin, the wind god, who also controls the weather. Raijin is also sometimes seen with Raiju, a beast made of lightning that can take various animal forms, especially a dog or wolf. Despite his destructive potential, Raijin's ability to bring rain is crucial for agriculture. Without him, drought would devastate the land. This duality of destruction and nourishment explains why he is also considered a protector of shrines and temples. In fact, a lightning strike on a crop was historically seen as a sign of an abundant harvest, thanks to Raijin's blessings.

Raijin features prominently in numerous myths, many of which date back centuries. One particularly frightening tale warns children to cover their belly buttons during storms, lest Raijin devour them. This myth likely stems from the belief that Raijin, born from supernatural forces, envies humans born naturally and covets their belly buttons.

The most significant legend involving Raijin is his role in protecting Japan from the Mongol invasions in the thirteenth century. This story reads like a mythical fantasy. Kublai Khan, the Mongol emperor, had already conquered much of East Asia and set his sights on Japan. In November 1274, the Mongol fleet approached Japan's shores, ready to invade. However, as the fleet neared, an overnight storm suddenly struck, pushing the Mongol ships back out to sea and decimating over half of their proud forces. This unexpected storm gave the Japanese much-needed time to strengthen their defenses.

Five years later, in 1281, the Mongols attempted another invasion with an even larger fleet. But, as they approached the Japanese coast, their eyes were immediately filled with horror as a powerful typhoon, known as a kamikaze or "divine wind," swept through, destroying nearly the entire Mongol fleet. This miraculous storm was attributed to Raijin and Fujin, who were hailed as the protectors of Japan. These divine storms were seen as manifestations of the kami's intervention, saving Japan from foreign conquest and reinforcing the belief in their protective powers.

Raijin's tales are not limited to his heroic acts. In one tale, Raijin caused widespread destruction with his storms. The relentless thunder and lightning brought chaos and suffering to the land, prompting the emperor to take decisive action. The emperor called upon Sugaru, a renowned god-catcher, to imprison Raijin and restore peace.

Sugaru, known for his cunning and bravery, approached Raijin with a petition, invoking the authority of the emperor. He requested Raijin to give himself up willingly and cease the storm. Raijin, in his defiant and mischievous manner, responded with a thunderous laugh, dismissing Sugaru's plea. Undeterred by Raijin's mocking, Sugaru turned to Kannon, the bodhisattva of mercy.

Kannon, moved by the suffering caused by Raijin's storms, intervened on behalf of Sugaru. She ordered Raijin to submit to Sugaru's request. Reluctantly, Raijin obeyed Kannon's command. With Raijin now subdued, Kannon delivered him to Sugaru, who tied him up in a sack and brought him before the emperor.

Under the control of Sugaru and the emperor, Raijin was forced to cease his destructive behavior. The once chaotic storms that had plagued the land were transformed into life-giving rains. Raijin's newfound restraint brought prosperity and bounty to Japan, ensuring that his storms would nourish the crops rather than destroy them.

Raijin's tales also extend to his interactions with other deities and his influence on human affairs. For instance, in the Sanjusangendo Temple and the Taiyuin Rinnoji Temple, Raijin is honored alongside his brother Fujin. At the Kaminarimon Gate of the Sensoji Temple, Raijin and Fujin stand guard, their statues made of wood with lacquer, gold leaf, paint, and crystal inlaid eyes. These sculptures are considered national treasures and symbolize the protective power of these kami.

In the Taiyuin Rinnoji Temple, Raijin and Fujin are depicted in the Niten-mon Gate, with Raijin holding his iconic drums and Fujin his wind bag. These statues, crafted with meticulous detail, serve as reminders of the kami's presence and their role in safeguarding the temples.

Raijin's presence in Japanese mythology and religious practices highlights the complex relationship between humans and the natural world. His ability to bring both destruction and life-giving rain makes him a symbol of nature's duality, respected and revered across Japan. Through his stories and depictions, Raijin continues to embody the powerful and unpredictable forces of nature, illustrating the delicate balance between chaos and order, destruction and creation.

Amaterasu, the Most Important Kami in Shintoism

Amaterasu, accompanied by Izanagi and Izanami on the right.[12]

Amaterasu, the sun goddess, is the most prominent and revered kami in Shinto. She occupies a central role in both Shinto and Japanese Buddhism, symbolizing light, purity, and order. As the goddess of the sun, Amaterasu is believed to illuminate all things, providing nourishment for life to flourish and marking the passage of time from day into night.

In Shintoism, the sun represents order and purity, two of the most fundamental concepts of the faith. The orderly movement of the sun across the sky, from sunrise to sunset, reflects the structured and harmonious nature of the universe. Amaterasu, as the embodiment of the sun, upholds this cosmic order, ensuring that all things in creation, from the heavens down to the denizens of Jigoku (hells), follow a divine hierarchy. This sense of order is mirrored in Japanese society, where social harmony and respect for hierarchy are deeply ingrained values.

Amaterasu's primary role as the sun goddess also makes her a provider of life. Her light dispels darkness and nurtures growth in all living creatures. In this capacity, she is venerated for her life-giving energy, which sustains the natural world and humans.

In Japanese Buddhism, Amaterasu is often incorporated into the pantheon of deities, symbolizing enlightenment and the all-seeing eye of wisdom. While she maintains her identity as a Shinto goddess, her attributes are harmoniously integrated into Buddhist practices, reflecting the syncretic nature of Japanese religion.

Amaterasu is typically depicted as a radiant and majestic figure. She is often shown with long flowing hair and wearing traditional regal garments. In some depictions, she holds a mirror, symbolizing self-reflection and truth. Her divine radiance is often illustrated with a halo or rays of light emanating from her, emphasizing her role as the source of illumination and purity.

Central to the story of Amaterasu is her tumultuous relationship with her brother, Susanoo, the storm god. Susanoo's reckless and destructive behavior often brought chaos and disorder, starkly contrasting with Amaterasu's embodiment of order and light. This sibling rivalry reached a climax in a famous tale that underscores Amaterasu's significance and the impact of her withdrawal from the world.

The popular tale begins with yet another episode of Susanoo's mischief. In a fit of rage, Susanoo rampaged through the heavens, destroying rice fields, defiling Amaterasu's sacred weaving hall, and frightening her attendants. He even went so far as to hurl a flayed horse through the roof of the weaving hall, causing one of Amaterasu's weavers to die from shock.

Heartbroken and furious, Amaterasu decided to withdraw from the world. She retreated into a cave called Ama-no-Iwato, sealing the entrance with a massive boulder. As the sun goddess hid away, the world was plunged into darkness. Without her light, crops failed, cold swept across the land, and chaos ensued. The absence of the sun caused immense suffering among both the gods and humans.

Desperate to bring light back to the world, the other gods convened a council to devise a plan to lure Amaterasu out of the cave. They gathered outside the cave and performed a series of rituals to coax her out. At the heart of their efforts was a grand celebration designed to catch Amaterasu's attention and curiosity.

First, they placed a large mirror on a tree directly outside the cave's entrance. This mirror, known as Yata-no-Kagami, was meant to reflect light and symbolize Amaterasu's brilliance. Next, they hung beautiful jewels and other treasures around the area, creating a scene of dazzling beauty. Then, the goddess of mirth, Ame-no-Uzume, took center stage. She overturned a large tub and began to dance atop it, stamping her feet rhythmically and creating a powerful beat. Her dance was wild and uninhibited, filled with joyous abandon. As she danced, Ame-no-Uzume began to disrobe, causing the other gods to roar with laughter and cheer.

Amaterasu, emerging from the cave.[13]

Hearing the commotion and laughter outside, Amaterasu's curiosity was piqued. *How could the others laugh and cheer while she was absent?* Amaterasu might have thought to herself. And so, unable to resist, she peeked out from the cave to see what was happening. When she did, she was immediately captivated by the reflection of her radiant beauty in the mirror and the joyous scene before her. The other gods seized this moment. The strong deity Ame-no-Tajikarao, who had been waiting in hiding, quickly pulled away the boulder blocking the entrance, allowing Amaterasu to step out fully.

As Amaterasu emerged, her light once again bathed the world in warmth and brilliance. The darkness receded, and life began to flourish once more. To ensure that such a crisis would never occur again, the gods devised measures to keep Susanoo in check, eventually banishing him from the heavens.

This legend of Amaterasu's retreat and return from the cave highlights her importance as the sun goddess. It underscores the balance between light and dark and the harmony that must be maintained for life to thrive. Through this tale, the reverence for Amaterasu and her central role in the cosmos is beautifully illustrated, reminding all of the delicate balance that sustains the world.

Indeed, Amaterasu's significance is not confined to mythology; her role is also woven into the very fabric of Japan's imperial tradition. According to tradition, the first emperor of Japan, Emperor Jimmu, was a direct descendant of Amaterasu. This divine ancestry established the imperial family's authority and reinforced its sacred status.

The connection between Amaterasu and the imperial family is symbolized by the Imperial Regalia of Japan, which includes three sacred treasures: the sword Kusanagi no Tsurugi, the jewel Yasakani no Magatama, and the mirror Yata no Kagami. The mirror, which played a crucial role in luring Amaterasu out of the cave, is particularly significant. It symbolizes wisdom and honesty, reflecting Amaterasu's radiant purity and the sun's illuminating power.

The Grand Shrine of Ise, or Ise Jingu, is the most important shrine dedicated to Amaterasu. Located in the Mie Prefecture, it is considered the spiritual heart of Shinto and the primary place of worship for the sun goddess. The shrine complex consists of two main shrines: the Inner Shrine (Naiku), dedicated to Amaterasu, and the Outer Shrine (Geku), dedicated to Toyouke Omikami, the goddess of agriculture and industry.

Ise Grand Shrine.[14]

Ise Jingu is renowned for its unique architectural style, known as shinmei-zukuri, characterized by simplicity and natural materials. The Inner Shrine houses the sacred mirror, Yata no Kagami, which is said to have been given to the first emperor by Amaterasu herself. This mirror is enshrined in the most sacred part of the Inner Shrine, where only the highest-ranking priests and the emperor may enter.

Interestingly, the shrine is rebuilt every twenty years in a ritual known as Shikinen Sengu, a tradition that has continued for over a millennium. This practice symbolizes renewal and the impermanence of all things, reflecting the cycles of nature that Amaterasu oversees. The old shrine is dismantled, and a new one is constructed on an adjacent site using fresh materials. This process involves transferring the sacred objects to the new shrine in a solemn and elaborate ceremony.

Celebrations and rituals dedicated to Amaterasu are an integral part of Japanese culture. One of the most significant festivals is the annual New Year's celebration, during which people pray for a prosperous and healthy year. The shrine's priests offer prayers and perform rituals to honor Amaterasu and seek her blessings for the coming year.

Another important festival is the Kannamesai, held every October, a harvest festival where the first fruits of the season are offered to Amaterasu. This festival reflects the goddess's role in providing nourishment and sustenance, emphasizing the gratitude of the people for the blessings of the harvest.

The Mikagura-uta, or sacred dances, are performed at Ise Jingu and other shrines to honor Amaterasu. These dances, accompanied by traditional music, are believed to please the goddess and ensure her continued favor. The rituals and ceremonies dedicated to Amaterasu are not only acts of worship but also expressions of cultural identity, linking the people to their divine heritage and the natural world.

Chapter 3 – The Samurai Spirit

It was just another normal day in ancient Japan. On one side of the village, the farmers could be seen working hard on their crops. On the other side, a lone samurai could be seen standing in a tranquil garden, practicing his swordsmanship. The morning mist clung to the ground, and the first rays of the sun reflected off the glistening blade of his katana. The samurai's movements were deliberate and precise, each swing of the sword echoing the discipline and honor that defined his very existence.

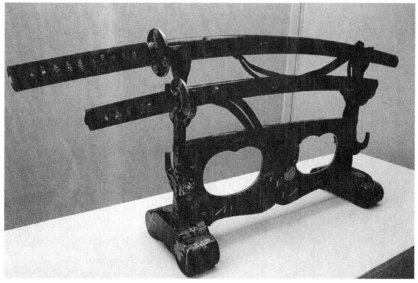

The daishō (a matching set of katana) owned by the Uesugi clan in the late Edo period.[15]

The katana, with its elegantly curved blade and razor-sharp edge, was more than just a weapon to the samurai. It was a symbol of honor, social status, and spiritual connection to the code of bushido—the way of the warrior. The samurai code was a philosophy that shaped the lives of these warriors. It required them to uphold a strict moral code, valuing loyalty to their lord and bravery in battle above all else. The samurai were expected to maintain their katana meticulously, regularly polishing and sharpening the blade to ensure it was always in perfect condition. This ritualistic care for their weapon was not just about functionality; it reflected their inner discipline and reverence for their role as warriors. The katana, often referred to as the soul of the samurai, embodied the spirit of bushido. Its gleaming surface symbolized purity and precision, while its lethal edge reminded the samurai of their duty to protect their honor and that of their master.

The origins of the samurai date back to ancient Japan, where they emerged as a distinct class of warriors during the Heian period (794-1185). The term "samurai" itself means "one who serves" and was initially used to describe the armed retainers of the nobility. The first samurai are thought to have been the bushi, or warrior aristocrats, who protected their lords' estates from bandits and rival clans. Over time, they evolved from mere protectors to the elite military class that dominated Japanese society.

Samurai in armor.[16]

The samurai played an important role in the history of Japan, serving as the military backbone of the various feudal lords and shoguns who ruled the country. They were not only warriors but also administrators and bureaucrats, ensuring the smooth functioning of their domains. The samurai went to war clad in elaborate armor, wielding their katanas with deadly precision. They fought on horseback and on foot, employing various martial techniques honed over years of rigorous training.

Central to the samurai's identity was their adherence to the shogunate, the military government that ruled Japan from the late twelfth century until the mid-nineteenth century. The shogunate was led by the shogun, a powerful military leader who commanded the loyalty of the samurai. In return for their service, the samurai were granted land and status, solidifying their position in the social hierarchy.

Of course, honor was paramount in samurai culture, and the ultimate expression of this was the practice of seppuku, or harakiri. This ritual suicide was performed to restore honor to a disgraced samurai or demonstrate loyalty to his lord. Seppuku involved the samurai disemboweling himself with his own sword, often followed by decapitation by a trusted assistant.

A samurai was indeed highly respected by the Japanese—pretty much like how the Europeans held their knights in high regard. To become a samurai was not at all easy. Their journey was rather perilous and teeming with formidable enemies left and right.

Miyamoto Musashi was one of Japan's most revered samurai whose story reverberated through the ages.

The Tale of Miyamoto Musashi

Miyamoto Musashi was a master swordsman and a figure of intense intrigue. It was not uncommon for samurai to adopt different names throughout their lives, reflecting their evolving status and identity. Musashi himself was initially known as Bennosuke. However, as he matured and his reputation grew, he came to be formally known as Miyamoto Musashi Genshin. The name "Miyamoto" is believed to reference the village where he was born, adding a layer of mystery and reverence to his persona.

The early life of Musashi is debated. Various theories suggest he was born in either the provinces of Harima or Mimasaka between 1582 and 1584. The question of whether Musashi's biological father was a samurai adds another layer of mystery to his origins. Despite these uncertainties, what is clear is that Musashi was adopted and displayed exceptional talent from a young age. His adoptive father, Shinmen Munisai, was a brave warrior in his own right and took it upon himself to train young Musashi in the ways of the sword.

Musashi's relationship with Munisai was tumultuous, marked by frequent arguments and clashes of will. The intensity of their conflicts grew over the years, and eventually, Musashi was cast out. This expulsion could have broken a lesser spirit, but Musashi was resolute. Determined to prove his worth, he went on a journey that would define his legacy. Musashi's first significant test of his skills came in the form of a duel at the tender age of thirteen. He challenged Arima Kihei, a samurai of the Shinto Ryu sword school. Kihei was known for his arrogance and eagerness to battle, though he was not particularly skilled. Despite this, challenging a samurai was a bold move, especially for someone as young as Musashi.

The duel was nearly called off due to Musashi's youth, but his determination could not be swayed. On the day of the duel, Musashi charged at Kihei with a fierce resolve that belied his years. Armed with a long staff, he deftly deflected Kihei's blade, knocking him to the ground. Musashi continued his assault, pummeling Kihei's head repeatedly—fourteen to fifteen times—until the ground was stained with blood and Kihei lay lifeless.

This brutal victory was a defining moment for Musashi, showcasing not only his raw talent but also his almost-divine spirit. This was only the beginning of a journey in which he would rise to legendary status, embodying the very essence of the samurai code.

From this moment onward, Musashi embarked on musha shugyō, a samurai's pilgrimage in which the warrior wandered across the land, practicing and honing his skills without the protection of his family or school. This journey, akin to the Chinese Youxia or European knight-errantry, was not only a test of skill but a way to earn a reputation. During these early years until 1600, Musashi was said to have fought and bested numerous opponents, each duel adding to his growing legend. At the age of sixteen, Musashi reunited with his adoptive father.

There is a popular belief that Musashi participated in the Great Battle of Sekigahara, a pivotal conflict that shaped Japan's future. While this remains speculative, during this period, Musashi and Munisai served a Daimyo aligned with Tokugawa Ieyasu, the first shogun of the Tokugawa shogunate. They fought in the eastern army's campaigns on Kyushu Island, providing Musashi with his first real taste of war.

As the Sekigahara conflict ended, Musashi turned his focus back to his swordsmanship. He traveled to Kyoto, where he sought out and challenged many of Japan's most skilled swordsmen. It was during this time, at the age of twenty-one, that he engaged in his famous duels against the Yoshioka school of swordsmanship, the official sword school for the shogun.

The confrontations with the Yoshioka school were defining moments in Musashi's life. He first defeated Seijuro Yoshioka, the head of the school, in a highly anticipated duel. Not long after, he faced Seijuro's younger brother, Denshichiro, and emerged victorious once again. The Yoshioka school, humiliated and desperate for revenge, laid an ambush for Musashi. Undeterred, Musashi faced the ambush with remarkable skill and composure, defeating a significant number of attackers. This series of victories marked the downfall of the Yoshioka house and solidified Musashi's legendary status.

In 1605, Musashi established his own sword school, initially named Enmei-ryu. Around this time, he also began writing one of his earliest works on swordsmanship, the Heidokyo, which he would continue to refine throughout his twenties. This period was characterized by intense learning and teaching, during which Musashi's techniques and philosophies began to spread, leaving a lasting impact on the martial traditions of Japan.

Musashi's journey across Japan did not end there; he continued to traverse the land, engaging in numerous legendary duels that further cemented his reputation. Among his most notable opponents were the Hozoin temple warrior monks, renowned for their mastery of Sojutsu (spear technique). The monks of Hozoin were formidable adversaries, their skills honed through rigorous training and spiritual discipline. Musashi's encounters with these monks were tests of his adaptability and ingenuity.

Another significant duel was against Muso Gonnosuke, the founder of Jojutsu Shindo Muso Ryu (staff techniques). Gonnosuke, a master of the bo staff, was said to be one of the few who managed to challenge Musashi and survive. According to legend, after an initial defeat, Gonnosuke developed a shorter staff technique, allowing for greater maneuverability and versatility.

Musashi also faced Shishido Baiken, a specialist in the kusarigama, a weapon consisting of a sickle attached to a chain with a heavy iron weight at the end. This weapon required a unique blend of offensive and defensive techniques, combining the reach of the chain with the lethality of the sickle. Musashi's victory over Baiken further demonstrated his unparalleled skill as a swordsman.

Despite the diversity of his opponents and the challenges they posed, Musashi never lost a duel. Each victory added to his growing legend and solidified his status as one of the greatest swordsmen of his time.

Among Musashi's many duels, the most legendary was his confrontation with Sasaki Kojiro, which took place on Ganryū-jima, an island between Honshū and Kyūshū, sometime around 1612. Sasaki Kojiro, also known as Demon of the Western Provinces, was the founder of the Ganryu school and a samurai of immense skill and renown. Known for his use of the nodachi, an extra-long sword, Kojiro's techniques and prowess were feared and respected throughout Japan. Unlike Musashi, who developed his own style through practical experience, Kojiro followed a long and prestigious lineage. He studied under Master Toda Seigen of the Chujo Ryu school and Kenemaki Jisai—a disciple of the famous sword master Itto Itosai, the founder of the Itto Ryu school, one of the most important swordsmanship styles in history. To put it simply, Kojiro was a challenging rival.

The duel between Musashi and Kojiro is undeniably one of the most famous in Japanese history. First, Musashi deliberately arrived late to unsettle his opponent. He kept Kojiro waiting on the beach for two hours past the appointed time. When Musashi finally arrived, he appeared calm and confident, carrying a wooden bokken he had fashioned from an oar during his boat ride to the island. This bokken was longer than a typical wooden sword, designed specifically to counter Kojiro's nodachi.

The duel began immediately upon Musashi's arrival. With intense focus, Musashi moved to strike in a single, decisive motion. He was well aware of Kojiro's preference for using the long reach of his sword to his advantage. Musashi's longer bokken allowed him to maintain distance while delivering a powerful blow. As Kojiro swung his nodachi, Musashi deflected the attack and struck Kojiro with precision, stunning him. Kojiro also landed a glancing blow on Musashi's forehead, but unfortunately for Kojiro, the strike was not fatal.

A depiction of the duel between Musashi (left) and Kojiro (right).[17]

The fight was quick and intense. After the initial exchange, Kojiro attempted a final, desperate strike from the ground, aiming at Musashi's legs. Musashi, anticipating the move, leaped to avoid the attack and delivered a fatal blow to Kojiro's hips, ending the duel. Kojiro's death marked the conclusion of one of the most storied encounters in samurai history, further immortalizing Musashi's legend.

The duel against Kojiro deeply affected Musashi. As he reflected on his victories, he was troubled by questions. Why had he won so many duels? Was it his physical strength? The weakness of his opponents? Or was it the will of the gods? These thoughts haunted him, driving him to spend the rest of his life searching for answers. This quest led him to refine his techniques into a style he called Niten Ichi Ryu, dedicating himself to passing on his knowledge to future generations.

Musashi's journey did not stop with swordsmanship; he explored the arts with the same dedication. He practiced Zen painting, creating minimalist and evocative artworks that mirrored his inner philosophy. He also took up sculpture, poetry, and architecture, finding solace and expression in these pursuits.

While he continued to fight in wars and accept duels, Musashi's focus shifted to teaching and developing his combat philosophy. He wrote extensively, aiming to share his insights with the world. In his later years, Musashi retreated to a cave, living as a hermit while pondering the deeper meanings of swordsmanship. It was in this solitude that he wrote his most famous work, the *Gorin no Sho* (*The Book of Five Rings*). This book, detailing his strategies and martial arts philosophy, became a cornerstone of his legacy.

Musashi never married but adopted two sons who went on to serve significant feudal lords. He died in 1645, but his legacy lived on. The *Gorin no Sho* and his life story cemented his status as a kensei, a "sword saint," a title reserved for warriors of legendary skill. Musashi's teachings and philosophy have inspired countless martial artists worldwide, making him one of history's greatest swordsmen.

The Revenge of the 47 Ronin

The Edo period, spanning from 1603 to 1868, is often heralded as a period of peace in Japan. Under the rule of the Tokugawa shogunate, Japan experienced unprecedented stability and prosperity. While many might imagine samurai during this era as constantly preparing for war, clad in armor with their katanas brandished, the reality was quite different.

With the absence of warfare, the life of a samurai shifted toward intellectual pursuits—chiefly poetry, calligraphy, and other arts. Although martial arts like Kenjutsu (swordsmanship) were still practiced, they became more ritualized, focusing less on combat and more on the preservation of tradition. Samurai transitioned into roles within administration and bureaucracy, living as civil servants dedicated to serving their feudal lords and, by extension, the shogun.

In April 1701, Edo Castle was abuzz with activity in preparation for a significant event. The rituals and protocols of the Edo period were taken very seriously, with intricate etiquette governing every aspect of ceremonial life. The event in question was a farewell ceremony for the emperor's representatives who had been staying at the castle. Kira Yoshinaka, a kōke, or master of ceremonies, was at the center of these preparations. Known for his strict adherence to protocol and his influential position, Kira's role was to ensure that all aspects of the ceremony were conducted flawlessly.

Among those involved in the ceremony was a young daimyo named Asano Naganori. Asano was tasked with receiving instructions from Kira on the necessary court etiquette. However, tensions quickly arose between them. Various accounts suggest different reasons for this animosity: some claimed Kira was displeased with the insufficient presents Asano offered, while others believed Kira's natural arrogance and corruption clashed with Asano's devoutly moral and Confucian principles. Asano, struggling to maintain his composure amidst Kira's insults, finally reached his breaking point.

Asano waited for Kira in the main corridor of the castle. When Kira appeared, Asano, unable to contain his rage any longer, slashed at him with his wakizashi (a short sword worn by samurai). Although Asano's first strike wounded Kira, his second strike missed, hitting a pillar instead. The commotion quickly attracted the castle guards, who secured Kira and restrained the enraged Asano.

A depiction of Asano's assault on Kira Yoshinaka.[18]

Attacking a shogunate official, especially within the shogun's residence, was a grave offense. Drawing a weapon inside Edo Castle was strictly forbidden, and samurai were only allowed to carry their wakizashi within the castle grounds. Additionally, shedding blood in the presence of the shogun and the emperor violated the Shinto belief in purity. Asano's actions were met with swift punishment: he was ordered to commit seppuku that very day. The shogun also stripped Asano's family of their lands and wealth, reducing his samurai retainers to ronin—masterless samurai.

To be a ronin was to live in disgrace, often viewed by society with suspicion and disdain. Unlike samurai, who had a lord to serve and a stable place in the social hierarchy, ronin wandered without purpose, often struggling to survive. This fate befell Asano retainers, but among them, forty-seven chose a path of vengeance.

Led by Oishi Yoshio, the forty-seven ronin plotted to kill Kira Yoshinaka. They knew Kira would be expecting retaliation, so they bided their time, waiting until he let his guard down. For two years, they lived as if they had abandoned their grudge. Oishi, to convince everyone of his supposed resignation, took to heavy drinking and public displays of debauchery. Their patience paid off, as Kira eventually relaxed his defenses.

In December 1702, the forty-seven ronin gathered at a secret location and finalized their plan. They vowed to avenge their master, making it clear that their mission was an act of katakiuchi (revenge). Oishi instructed his men to avoid harming women, children, and the helpless. Their goal was to kill Kira and place his severed head on Asano's tomb before surrendering themselves to face their fate.

Then, on a cold December night, the forty-six ronin (one was sent on another mission) stormed Kira's residence. One climbed onto the roof to loudly announce their intentions, ensuring that the public knew they were not robbers or murderers but masterless samurai seeking revenge. Many of those who despised Kira silently cheered and did nothing to impede the ronin.

Kira, hearing the commotion, attempted to flee and hide with his wife and female servants. His retainers fought valiantly, but the ronin were relentless. Sixteen of Kira's men were killed and another twenty-two wounded. Kira himself was nowhere to be found. Oishi, checking Kira's bed and finding it still warm, deduced that Kira was close by. The ronin eventually discovered a hidden courtyard where Kira had taken refuge.

Upon finding Kira, Oishi respectfully addressed him, offering him the chance to die honorably by seppuku. Oishi even offered to act as Kira's kaishakunin (second), the one who would decapitate him to minimize his suffering. Kira remained speechless. Seeing no other option, Oishi ordered his men to pin Kira down. He was killed with a dagger—the same one Asano had used for his seppuku.

The ronin washed Kira's severed head in a well before placing it on Asano's tomb alongside the dagger. They offered prayers and left their remaining money with the temple's abbot, asking for their bodies to be decently buried and prayers to be offered for their souls. They then turned themselves in, fully expecting the death sentence.

As anticipated, the shogun sentenced the forty-six ronin to death. However, recognizing their act of loyalty and honor, they were allowed to commit seppuku rather than face execution as common criminals. The youngest among them was only sixteen years old. The forty-seventh ronin, Terasaka Kichiemon, returned and was later pardoned. The forty-six ronin were buried at Sengaku-ji, in front of their master's tomb.

The graves of the ronin at Sengaku-ji.[19]

The tale of the forty-seven ronin quickly became famous and remains one of Japan's most enduring stories, conveying the message of the samurai's undying loyalty and honor. The story, known as "Chūshingura" (The Treasury of Loyal Retainers), has been retold in countless plays, books, and films, each time reinforcing the ideals of bushido—the way of the warrior. The ronin's act of avenging their master and willingly facing death to uphold their honor exemplifies the deepest values of the samurai: loyalty to one's lord, the importance of honor, and the willingness to sacrifice everything for one's principles.

Even today, the graves of the forty-seven ronin at Sengaku-ji Temple are a site of pilgrimage. Visitors come to pay their respects and honor the memory of these loyal samurai. The annual festival held at Sengaku-ji on December 14, commemorating the day the ronin avenged their master, draws people from all over Japan and beyond. This festival is a celebration of the virtues that the forty-seven ronin embodied and that continue to resonate in Japanese culture.

Chapter 4 – Folktales of Love and Destiny

Once upon a time, in the verdant countryside of ancient Japan, there lived an elderly bamboo cutter named Taketori no Okina. Each day, he ventured into the thick bamboo groves, his sharp axe gleaming under the sunlight as he meticulously cut and gathered the slender stalks. His humble life was filled with the rhythmic sounds of nature and the soft rustle of bamboo leaves, but there was a void in his heart, for he and his wife, Asagao, had no children.

One tranquil morning, as the golden rays of the sun pierced through the emerald canopy, Taketori no Okina noticed an extraordinary glow emanating from a bamboo stalk. Mesmerized, he approached the luminous plant and, with great care, split it open. To his astonishment, nestled inside the stalk was a tiny, radiant baby girl, no larger than his thumb. Her delicate features and ethereal glow filled Taketori no Okina's heart with joy and wonder. Believing her to be a divine gift, he gently cradled the tiny girl and brought her home to his wife.

Asagao was equally enchanted by the miraculous child. Together, they named her Kaguya-hime, meaning "radiant princess." Miraculously, within just a few days, Kaguya-hime grew from a tiny infant to a beautiful young woman, her beauty unmatched by any other. Her hair shimmered like the midnight sky, and her eyes sparkled like the brightest stars. The bamboo cutter and his wife cherished her deeply, their lives now brimming with happiness and love.

Strangely, after Kaguya-hime came into their lives, every time Taketori no Okina cut the bamboo, he found nuggets of gold within the stalks. Soon, the once humble couple became wealthy, their home filled with treasures and their hearts with gratitude for the extraordinary gift bestowed upon them.

Kaguya-hime's beauty soon became legendary, and word of the celestial maiden spread far and wide. Noblemen from distant lands traveled to the bamboo cutter's modest home, each hoping to win her hand in marriage. Five princes, each renowned for their wealth and status, were the most persistent suitors. Headstrong to marry the beautiful Kaguya-hime, these suitors met Taketori no Okina one day, hoping they could persuade his radiant daughter into accepting one of their marriage proposals. Nevertheless, Kaguya-hime remained uninterested. But, not planning on disappointing her father, Kaguya-hime agreed to marry any one of the suitors who successfully fulfilled her rather impossible condition.

The first prince was asked to retrieve the stone begging bowl of the Buddha. Determined, he set off on the long journey but soon realized the task was impossible. Desperate, he found an old bowl from a local temple and tried to pass it off as the true relic. However, Kaguya-hime saw through his deception—the bowl did not have a certain glow—and sent him away in shame.

The second prince was tasked with finding a branch from the mythical island of Horai, made of gold and adorned with jeweled fruits. He hired an exceptionally skillful craftsman to create a magnificent fake branch, hoping to deceive Kaguya-hime. The beautiful maiden was slightly surprised when he presented the branch, but the prince's deceit was revealed when Kaguya-hime received a messenger sent by the craftsman, asking for payment.

The third prince was to obtain a robe made from the fire-rat's fur, which could not be burned. He traveled to distant lands, spending a fortune, only to return with an ordinary robe. When Kaguya-hime tested the robe by setting it on fire, it burned to ashes, and the prince departed in defeat.

The fourth prince was asked to bring back a colored jewel from a dragon's neck. He went on a journey across the seas and was later forced to face the merciless storm. Afraid for his life, the prince decided to abandon the mission. As for the fifth prince, he faced a grimmer fate.

Tasked to fetch a cowry shell born from swallows, the undeterred prince went and searched tirelessly for a swallow's nest. He found one, but it was high above the ground. The prince tried to reach for it but unfortunately fell to his death.

Later, the emperor, having heard of Kaguya-hime's unmatched beauty, also decided to venture to the outskirts, hoping he could catch a glimpse of the legendary maiden. Unsurprisingly, upon laying eyes on Kaguya-hime, the emperor was immediately captivated by her grace and beauty. Almost immediately, he sought her hand in marriage, offering her the luxuries and power of his court. But Kaguya-hime, with a heavy heart, refused. She explained that she was not from his country; the marriage was impossible. However, the two remained in contact. For three years, they continued to send each other letters.

Nevertheless, Kaguya-hime remained lonely and wistful. Then came summer, when she would often gaze at the moon with longing. Her eyes filled with sadness that her foster parents could not understand. As the seasons changed and summer gave way to autumn, Kaguya-hime's melancholy deepened. One evening, under the soft glow of the moon, she finally revealed to Taketori no Okina and Asagao that she was not of this world but a princess from the Moon Kingdom. She had been sent to Earth as a punishment for a certain wrongdoing that she refused to explain. The gold that they receive was sent from the heavens as some form of payment for the princess's upkeep. This punishment had come to an end, and she must return to where she belonged.

Her foster parents were devastated by the revelation, unable to fathom losing their beloved daughter. They pleaded with her to stay, but Kaguya-hime's fate was sealed. She assured them that she would always cherish the love and care they had shown her. Meanwhile, the news soon reached the emperor, who vowed to keep her on Earth. When Kaguya-hime revealed that her time on Earth was nearing its end, the emperor wasted no time. He deployed his most loyal guards to surround her house on the night of her departure, determined to thwart the celestial beings who would come to take her back.

On that fateful night when the full moon bathed the land in its silvery light, celestial beings descended from the heavens in a resplendent chariot. Dressed in shimmering robes, they approached Kaguya-hime, who was now adorned in a radiant garment that enhanced her otherworldly beauty. The emperor's guards, brave and resolute, formed a barrier around the house, but they were no match for the celestial beings. The ethereal figures effortlessly bypassed the guards, their divine presence overwhelming all resistance.

Taketori no Okina and Asagao wept as they watched their beloved daughter bid them farewell, her luminous eyes filled with tears of gratitude and sorrow. Kaguya-hime wrote moving letters of farewell to her family and to the emperor, expressing her deep love and gratitude for their kindness. She also left a small bottle with the Elixir of Life for the emperor, a final gift to the one who had loved her so dearly.

As Kaguya-hime ascended to the sky, she looked back at the couple who had given her a life of love and happiness. Her celestial entourage then draped a feather robe around her, erasing all her earthly memories as she ascended to the moon, heading straight to Tsuki no Miyako (the Capital of the Moon).

Kaguya-hime ascending to the moon.[20]

The emperor, devastated by Kaguya-hime's departure, read her letter and felt an overwhelming sense of loss. Distraught, he wrote her a heartfelt letter, expressing his undying love and sorrow. He then ordered his men to climb to the top of the tallest mountain in Japan and burn the letter, hoping that the smoke would carry his words and feelings to Kaguya-hime in the heavens. The Elixir of Life was also burned as the emperor did not wish to reach immortality without the princess by his side. From that day on, it was said that the plume of smoke from the mountain symbolized the emperor's eternal love and longing for Kaguya-hime. Legend also has it that the word for immortality (fushi) became the mountain's name: Mount Fuji.

The tale of the bamboo cutter and his moon princess, Kaguya-hime, was written during the Heian period—possibly in the late ninth or early tenth century, making it one of the oldest folktales ever recorded. It immediately became a cherished story passed down through generations. The tale reminds all who heard it of the beauty of love, sacrifice, and the ethereal magic that sometimes graces the world.

This is not the only tale that speaks of love. Another popular legend that blends human emotions with mystical elements is the story of Tsuru Nyōbō (The Crane Wife).

The Tale of the Crane Wife

The story takes place in a small village, home to a certain young man. He was a kind-hearted person, living a simple life in a modest cottage at the edge of a dense forest. One crisp autumn day, as the young man walked through the forest to gather firewood, he heard a faint, sorrowful cry. Following the sound, he discovered a beautiful crane with an arrow piercing its wing. The crane's pristine white feathers were stained with blood, and its eyes pleaded for mercy.

Moved with compassion, the young man carefully removed the arrow. "You have to be careful of the hunters next time," he softly said while tending to the crane's wounds.

The grateful bird gazed at him with deep, intelligent eyes before spreading its majestic wings and soaring into the sky. The young man watched the crane disappear into the distance, his heart warmed by the knowledge that he had saved a life.

That night, as the wind rustled through the trees and leaves fell softly to the ground, there was a gentle knock on the young man's door. When he opened it, he found a stunning young woman standing on his doorstep. She introduced herself as his wife. Though confused, the young man explained that he had no wealth to support them both. The woman reassured him, saying she had brought a sack of rice large enough to feed them both.

To the young man's amazement, the rice never depleted, and they were never left hungry. As the days passed, they grew closer, and the young man found himself captivated by her gentle demeanor and mysterious beauty. One evening, under the soft glow of the hearth, the woman asked the young man to build her a weaving room. Despite his

42

modest means, he set to work and soon had a small room ready for her.

Before she began her weaving, the young man's wife made him swear never to peek at her while she worked. She closed herself in the room, and the young man waited outside, listening to the steady clatter of the loom. Days passed. At last, after seven days, the sound ceased. His wife, now frail and thin, emerged from the room holding the most exquisite cloth he had ever seen.

The following day, the young man took the fabric to the village market, where it fetched a very high price. Their lives improved, and their once simple home became cozy and warm. Yet, the young man's curiosity kept growing. How could his wife create such remarkable fabrics?

One night, unable to resist any longer, he tiptoed to the room where his wife worked. Peering through a tiny crack in the door, he was stunned to see a large crane at the loom, pulling feathers from its own body to weave into the fabric. As he gasped in surprise, the crane transformed back into his wife, who turned to him with tears in her eyes.

"You have broken your vow," she said sorrowfully. "I am the crane you rescued, and I became your wife to repay your kindness. But now that you have seen my true form, I must leave."

Devastated, the young man pleaded with her to stay, but it was too late. She wept as she turned back into the crane, spread her wings, and with a sorrowful cry, flew off into the night. The young man watched her vanish into the darkness, his heart aching with regret and sadness. But, before she left, the crane had given the young man one last piece of fabric to remember her by. He clutched the beautiful cloth, knowing it was her final gift to him.

From that day forward, the young man often wandered through the forest, hoping to glimpse the crane he had once saved and loved. Though he never saw her again, he would sometimes hear a sorrowful cry echoing among the trees, a reminder of the love he had lost because of his broken promise.

The tale of The Crane Wife imparts important lessons. It shows that true love is generous and kind but also emphasizes the importance of keeping promises. Curiosity can lead to heartache, and sometimes it's best to trust and respect the privacy of those we care about. The young man's sorrowful experience serves as a reminder to cherish and honor the trust others place in us.

The Tale of the Star-Crossed Lovers

This next tale is a cherished legend that paints the night sky with a story of love and longing. Represented by the stars Vega and Altair, these celestial lovers are separated by the Milky Way.

In the heavens far from our world, there was once an enchanting weaver named Orihime. She was not merely an ordinary weaver; Orihime was, in fact, a princess, the daughter of the God of the Sky. Most of the time, Orihime could be seen working diligently at her loom by the banks of the Amanogawa (the River of Heaven), which is known to us today as the Milky Way. With her celestial skills, her weavings were always so exquisite that they shone like the brightest stars themselves.

Despite her skill and dedication, Orihime was always lonely. She longed for companionship and love, but her constant weaving left her no time for such pursuits. Seeing his daughter's sadness, the God of the Sky decided to help. He introduced her to Hikoboshi, a handsome young cowherd who lived on the opposite side of the Amanogawa. Hikoboshi was known for his kindness and his devotion to his herd of celestial cows.

When Orihime and Hikoboshi met, it was love at first sight. They were instantly drawn to each other, and soon they were inseparable. Their love blossomed, and for a time, both were blissfully happy. They spent every moment they could together—laughing, talking, and enjoying each other's company.

However, their newfound happiness came with a price. Orihime's weaving was neglected, Hikoboshi's cows wandered unattended, and chaos threatened the celestial order. Orihime's father, noticing the disorder, was greatly displeased. And so, he summoned Orihime and Hikoboshi and decreed that they must be separated by the Amanogawa as punishment for their neglect.

Heartbroken, Orihime and Hikoboshi were placed on opposite sides of the Milky Way, forbidden to see each other. The separation was unbearable, and both spent their days gazing longingly across the river of stars, their hearts aching with sorrow. The sadness eventually grew so strong that it attracted the attention of the God of the Sky. Seeing his daughter's misery and moved by her tears, Orihime's father decided to show mercy.

He allowed Orihime and Hikoboshi to meet once a year on the seventh day of the seventh month—this is known as Tanabata, which means "Evening of the Seventh." There was, however, a condition; they could only meet if they agreed to work hard and complete their duties throughout the rest of the year. Perhaps desperately longing for each other's company, the two lovers quickly agreed on the terms. They continued to complete their duties. Following this, chaos disappeared from the heavens.

When the day finally came, the two were elated. It was the first day that they were to be reunited after a full year. However, they soon found the river to be too difficult to cross. Orihime was immediately consumed by sorrow. But as before, her sadness soon attracted the attention of others. A flock of magpies came to help the two lovers reunite. They made a bridge for Orihime to cross the river, allowing her to embrace Hikoboshi once again. The pair cherished every moment of their reunion, perhaps holding each other close and sharing stories of their time apart. The sight of their love rekindled brought hope and happiness to all other celestial beings. However, it is said that the magpies could only assist them on their yearly journey if the day was clear. If rain came on the date, the two lovers must wait another year to be reunited.

Today, the story of Orihime and Hikoboshi is celebrated with the Tanabata festival. People write their wishes on colorful strips of paper called tanzaku and hang them on bamboo trees, creating beautiful wish trees. On the following day, these decorated trees are floated on a river or in the ocean and burned as an offering, carrying the wishes to the heavens.

A bamboo tree full of tanzaku.[21]

Throughout Japan, Tanabata is marked by various celebrations. The streets come alive with parades, food stalls, and colorful decorations. People of all ages participate in the festivities, enjoying traditional foods, music, and games. Fireworks light up the night sky, mirroring the joy of the heavenly reunion and adding to the magical atmosphere of the festival.

The Tanabata festival is a time for people to come together and celebrate love, hope, and the beauty of the stars. Families and friends gather to share the story of Orihime and Hikoboshi, teaching the next generation about the power of love and the importance of perseverance and hard work. As they gaze up at the Milky Way, they imagine the celestial lovers meeting on their bridge of magpies, their love shining brightly across the heavens.

Through the festival of Tanabata, the tale of Orihime and Hikoboshi is immortalized. It serves as a timeless reminder of love's enduring strength, the value of dedication, and the beauty of the stars that guide us.

The Harrowing Tale of Kiyohime and Anchin

Love, a powerful and beautiful emotion, can sometimes grow into an all-consuming obsession. When love turns into an unhealthy fixation, it can drive people to unimaginable lengths, causing pain and suffering for both the lover and the beloved. One such harrowing tale from Japanese folklore that vividly illustrates this transformation is the story of Anchin and Kiyohime. This legend reveals the dark side of love turned obsession.

The setting of this daunting legend was the ancient province of Kii, where there lived a beautiful young woman named Kiyohime. The daughter of an official of the Manago manor, she was known for her grace and beauty. One day, a traveling monk named Anchin arrived at her father's manor. Anchin was a handsome and devout monk on a pilgrimage to a sacred temple. When Kiyohime saw him, she immediately fell deeply in love.

"Welcome, honored monk," Kiyohime greeted, her eyes shining with admiration. "May I offer you food and rest for your journey?"

Anchin accepted her hospitality graciously, unaware of the growing affection Kiyohime harbored for him. During his stay at the manor, they spent time talking, and Kiyohime's feelings for Anchin intensified. When it was time for Anchin to continue his journey, Kiyohime pleaded with him to stay longer, but he gently refused.

"Kiyohime, I must fulfill my pilgrimage," Anchin explained, sensing her attachment. "It is my duty to the temple and to my faith. I will return to you the very moment I'm done with my responsibilities."

Heartbroken but hopeful, Kiyohime watched him leave, believing he would return. As Anchin continued his pilgrimage, he became increasingly aware of the inappropriateness of Kiyohime's affections. He resolved to avoid her on his return journey, fearing the consequences of her obsession.

Months later, Anchin returned to the province of Kii, taking a different route to avoid Kiyohime. However, she learned of his return and was determined to see him again. She waited by the roadside, hoping to intercept him. When Anchin saw her, he panicked and fled, seeking refuge in a nearby temple.

"Kiyohime, please understand," Anchin pleaded as he ran. "I am a monk, and I cannot return your love."

Kiyohime on the banks of the Hidaka River.[22]

Devastated by his rejection and consumed by her desire, Kiyohime's heartbreak twisted into rage. She pursued Anchin relentlessly. Anchin, on the other hand, had successfully crossed the Hidaka River and specifically told the boatman to not ferry Kiyohime. And so, when the enraged maiden arrived at the edge of the river, the boatman told her to turn back. Not ready to let the monk go, Kiyohime jumped into the river. It was at this moment that a harrowing transformation took place. The body of the once beautiful maiden contorted, and in the blink of an eye, she transformed into a monstrous serpent, driven by a single-minded obsession to get Anchin.

Anchin was beyond terrified. He ran as fast as he could to the Dōjō-ji. Wrestling with panic, Anchin sought help from the priest of Dōjō-ji. Here, sources vary; some claim that the priests at the temple did not believe Anchin's story, while others suggest they took his words seriously. Nevertheless, Anchin eventually found a hiding spot. He was said to have been hiding under the gigantic temple bell, hoping his life could be spared from the vengeful serpent. However, Kiyohime, in her new form, had a rather heightened sense of smell. She could easily smell the terrified monk's scent and pinpoint his hiding spot. Without wasting time, she coiled around the bell, her scales scraping against the metal. She breathed fire upon it, heating the bell until it glowed red-hot.

A section of a scroll depicting Kiyohime as a serpent, burning the bell.[23]

Anchin, trapped inside, slowly began to feel the searing heat and knew he could not escape his fate. The only thing he could do was to pray for the last time, his trembling voice mingling with the desperate hisses of the serpent outside. In a final agonizing moment, the flames consumed him, and the bell shattered from the intense heat. Kiyohime, realizing what she had done, let out a mournful wail that echoed through the temple grounds. Her monstrous form collapsed, and she wept bitterly over the charred remains of the monk she had loved. As she could no longer bear her sorrow, Kiyohime fled to the river, where she ended her own life.

Anchin and Kiyohime's tragic end serves as a reminder of the destructive power of unchecked emotions. Kiyohime's love, which turned into an all-consuming obsession, led to her transformation into a creature of wrath and vengeance. Anchin's attempts to escape only fueled her rage, culminating in a heartbreaking and fiery demise for both.

Chapter 5 – Yokai and Supernatural Creatures

The streets of the Edo-period town were shrouded in an eerie silence as the moon cast its pale glow over the narrow lanes. The lanterns flickered softly, their light barely cutting through the thick darkness. A lone man—let us call him Sato—made his way home after a long day of work. The stillness of the night was unsettling, and the quiet was so profound that it seemed to amplify the sound of his own footsteps.

As Sato walked, a prickling sensation crawled up his spine. He felt the uncanny impression that he was being followed. Glancing around, he saw nothing but shadows dancing on the walls and the occasional rustling of leaves in the wind. The feeling persisted, growing stronger with each step, until he could no longer ignore it. Gathering his courage, he decided to turn around and confront whatever was behind him.

There, standing in the middle of the deserted street, was a small boy. The boy was more than half the size of an average man and wore a large bamboo hat that obscured much of his face. He looked lonely, a solitary figure in the night. In his hands, he held a dish with a large block of tofu, a Japanese maple leaf stamped on the side. The boy resembled a typical tofu seller, a common sight during the day, yet something about him filled Sato with unease.

"Good evening," the boy said in a soft voice, extending the dish towards Sato. "Would you like some tofu?"

Sato hesitated but then accepted the offering. The boy's eyes, barely visible under the brim of the hat, seemed to glimmer with a strange light. Thanking the boy, Sato quickly made his way home, eager to escape the unsettling encounter.

Once home, Sato examined the tofu. It appeared ordinary, and with a shrug, he decided to eat it. The tofu tasted rather bland and had no flavor at all. "Just an ordinary tofu," Sato thought to himself, feeling a sense of relief. Little did he know, he was lucky.

A depiction of Tōfu-kozō.[24]

In other circumstances, eating the tofu given by Tōfu-kozō could lead to far worse outcomes. For the unfortunate, mold would spread across the jiggly white surface of the tofu as they ate it. Sometimes, those who consumed the mold without noticing it would find it growing within their bodies, eventually leading to their demise. Such occurrences were rare, as Tōfu-kozō did not usually make humans their opponents. In fact, these yokai (supernatural creatures and spirits) were frequently depicted as amicable, timid, and humorous characters. They were often teased by other yokai for being weak and were known to serve as errand runners for stronger yokai.

Tōfu-kozō, with his endearing yet eerie presence, was a unique yokai. But, to understand him fully, it is essential to delve into what yokai represent in Japanese beliefs. Each type of yokai have their own unique characteristics and stories. They can be malevolent, benevolent, or merely mischievous, embodying the fears, curiosities, and the unknown aspects of human life. The origins of yokai are deeply rooted in ancient Japanese beliefs and the folklore of the countryside, where people lived in close harmony with nature.

However, the story of Tōfu-kozō is different. This yokai was born in the bustling cities during the Edo period. Tofu had arrived from China early in Japan's history during the Nara or Heian period, but it was not until the Edo period that tofu became popular. Initially enjoyed by the elites, tofu gradually became a staple food for all classes.

During this period, many reported encountering Tōfu-kozō. Each description varied slightly, but the essence remained the same. Some claimed that Tōfu-kozō was a shy creature, often tiptoeing behind those wandering the empty streets at night. Others said he preferred to appear during the rain. The drawings of Tōfu-kozō also varied. While many depicted him as a rather adorable young boy, others described him as having only one large eye or a long tongue. Despite these differences, most accounts agreed that Tōfu-kozō was neither malevolent nor evil.

Interestingly, Tōfu-kozō was often seen wearing red, a color believed by ancient Japanese to have the power to ward off evil. This detail connects him to other yokai and spirits in Japanese folklore, such as Hosogami, the smallpox spirit.

How the Ancient Japanese Warded Off the Smallpox Demon

The history of smallpox in Japan is as harrowing as it is fascinating. The disease first struck the archipelago in the eighth century during the Nara period. It is believed that smallpox arrived via trade routes from the Korean Peninsula and China, spreading rapidly through the population. The epidemic of 735-737 CE was particularly devastating, wiping out a significant portion of the Japanese population and altering the course of the nation's history.

Before the advent of medical science and the understanding of diseases, the ancient Japanese believed that smallpox was brought by a malevolent spirit known as Hosogami. This smallpox demon was thought to travel through the land, spreading the disease and wreaking havoc among the people. Hosogami was feared greatly, and various rituals and practices were developed to ward off this dreaded spirit.

One of the primary means of protection against Hosogami was the color red. It was widely believed that red had the power to repel evil spirits and negative influences. In the context of smallpox, families would dress their sick in red garments, decorate their homes with red objects, and even paint red symbols on their walls. The hope was that this vibrant color would drive away Hosogami and prevent the spread of disease.

In addition to the use of red, the ancient Japanese employed various other methods to protect themselves from Hosogami. Some believed that by pleasing the smallpox demon, they could avert the disease. As a result, they set up small shrines dedicated to Hosogami, offering prayers and sacrifices to pacify the spirit. These shrines were often adorned with red paper streamers called shide, which were believed to further enhance their protective power.

Another common practice involved tying straw ropes, known as shimenawa, around the house. These ropes, also adorned with shide, were traditionally used to mark sacred spaces and ward off evil spirits. By placing shimenawa around their homes, people hoped to create a protective barrier that would keep Hosogami at bay.

One of the most famous stories involving Hosogami is that of Minamoto no Tametomo. Tametomo was a legendary samurai of the late Heian period, renowned for his archery skills and adventurous life. According to folklore, Tametomo once encountered Hosogami and, using his extraordinary abilities, chased off the demon and protected the people from smallpox.

Minamoto no Tametomo was also a figure of great cultural significance. His actions against Hosogami were symbolic of the eternal struggle between humans and the supernatural forces that sought to harm them. By standing up to Hosogami, Tametomo became a symbol of hope and resilience.

Minamoto no Tametomo casting off the smallpox demon.[25]

The fear of smallpox and the reverence for Hosogami also led to various local festivals and rituals aimed at preventing outbreaks. In some regions, entire villages would participate in purification rites, offering prayers and performing dances to appease the spirit. These communal activities not only served a spiritual purpose but also strengthened social bonds and provided a sense of collective security in the face of an invisible threat.

As medical knowledge advanced and the true nature of smallpox became understood, the belief in Hosogami gradually faded. However, the cultural practices and folklore surrounding the smallpox spirit left a lasting impact on Japanese society. The use of red as a protective color, the rituals of purification, and the stories of heroic figures like Minamoto no Tametomo remain embedded in the cultural memory. The tale of Hosogami illustrates the complex interplay between superstition, religion, and medicine in ancient Japan. It shows how people sought to make sense of the unknown and protect themselves through a blend of practical and spiritual means.

The Legend of the Nine-Tailed Fox

Another legendary figure in the world of yokai is the kitsune, a shape-shifting fox spirit renowned in Japanese folklore for its cunning and trickery. Among the most famous of these tales is that of Tamamo no Mae, the notorious Nine-Tailed Fox.

The story begins with a married couple who discover an abandoned baby girl. Some versions of the tale say they found her in the woods, while others claim she was left on the streets. The couple, childless and longing for a family, took the infant in and named her Mizukume. They showered her with love and care, and as the years passed, Mizukume grew into an extraordinarily beautiful and intelligent girl.

By the age of seven, Mizukume had already shown remarkable talent. She could read and compose poetry, charming everyone with her brilliance and grace. Her reputation soon spread, and she was invited to perform her poetry before the reigning emperor, Emperor Toba.

Mizukume's performance was nothing short of mesmerizing. The emperor was captivated by her eloquence and beauty. "Such a remarkable child," Emperor Toba mused, his eyes never leaving her. "She must be brought to court."

And so, Mizukume was taken to the imperial court, where she was given the name Tamamo no Mae. She quickly became a favorite among the courtiers. Mothers wished their children were more like her, and everyone in court adored her company. Her intelligence shone brightly, especially when scholars tested her knowledge with difficult questions, all of which she answered with ease. Her growing popularity caught the emperor's attention once more, and he spent every free moment in her presence.

As Tamamo no Mae grew into a fine maiden, she became the emperor's consort. They were inseparable, and Emperor Toba found great joy in her company. However, this happiness was not to last. Suddenly, the emperor fell mysteriously ill. His condition worsened day by day, baffling the court physicians, who could find no cure.

Only one thing seemed unusual: despite the emperor's grave condition, Tamamo no Mae did not appear particularly distressed. Her calm demeanor amidst the crisis raised suspicions among the courtiers.

In desperation, the court summoned Abe no Yasunari, an onmyōji known for his expertise in divination and the supernatural. Abe no Yasunari performed several rituals to diagnose the problem. He soon declared that the emperor was not suffering from a natural illness but was cursed by an evil spirit. Alarmed by this revelation, the court summoned priests from across the land to pray at the palace, hoping to ward off the malevolent force. Despite their efforts, the emperor's condition continued to deteriorate.

Growing ever more restless and desperate, the court pleaded with Abe no Yasunari to perform another ritual. This time, the onmyōji's findings shocked everyone: the culprit behind the emperor's illness was none other than Tamamo no Mae. He declared that she was a kitsune and was using her magic to slowly kill the emperor.

"Impossible!" the courtiers exclaimed. "Tamamo no Mae cannot be the cause of this!"

The emperor himself, though weakened, was deeply hurt by the accusation. "Tamamo," he whispered, "could this be true?"

The court agreed to perform a test devised by Abe no Yasunari to reveal Tamamo no Mae's true form. The onmyōji explained that during a sacred ritual, no evil spirit could maintain a disguise and would be forced to reveal itself. At first, Tamamo no Mae hesitated, but under pressure from the court, she agreed to participate.

Tamamo no Mae transforming into the nine-tailed fox.[26]

As the ritual commenced, the air grew tense. Chanting priests surrounded Tamamo no Mae, and the atmosphere crackled with spiritual energy. Suddenly, Tamamo no Mae began to writhe and twist, her form changing before their very eyes. In a horrifying transformation, the beautiful maiden morphed into a fearsome nine-tailed fox.

The courtiers gasped in terror, and the emperor's eyes widened in disbelief. The kitsune, now fully exposed, let out a fierce cry before leaping out of a nearby window and disappearing into the night. Heartbroken, the emperor knew he had to deal with the creature that had once been his beloved consort. Reports soon flooded in from across the country of women and children mysteriously disappearing, presumably taken by the vengeful fox. Determined to protect his people, the emperor summoned his two best warriors, Kazusanosuke and Miuranosuke, to hunt down and eliminate the kitsune.

The two warriors pursued Tamamo no Mae relentlessly. Despite her cunning and ability to outsmart them several times, Kazusanosuke and Miuranosuke's determination never wavered. After rigorous training and countless encounters, they finally managed to corner her. With precise aim, they fired two arrows that struck the kitsune.

This, however, was not the last of Tamamo no Mae. After her defeat, her spirit was said to be trapped in a boulder known as Sessho-seki, or the Killing Stone. Anyone foolish enough to touch the boulder was said to have faced death. This boulder existed for centuries, but in 2022, it mysteriously cracked open, leading many to believe that Tamamo no Mae's spirit had been freed.

Sessho-seki split in half.[27]

Despite her defeat, Emperor Toba's fate was also sealed: he succumbed to his illness not long after. The turmoil surrounding his court and the chaos following Tamamo no Mae's exposure contributed to the unrest that eventually led to the Genpei War, a civil war that changed the course of Japanese history.

The tale of Tamamo no Mae is a great lesson of how appearances can be deceiving and how power and beauty can mask darker intentions. This legendary kitsune, with her enchanting disguise and malevolent heart, remains one of the most captivating and cautionary figures in Japanese folklore. Today, her legend is referenced in movies, books, and various forms of media, keeping her story alive and relevant.

Her influence is not confined to Japan. In Chinese history, Tamamo no Mae appears as Da Ji, the notorious concubine of King Zhou of

Shang. Much like in Japan, Da Ji's beauty hid a cruel and malevolent nature that brought great misfortune to the Shang dynasty, leading to its downfall. Her story is eerily like that of Tamamo no Mae, highlighting the universal themes of deception and the destructive power of unchecked desires.

The Honorable Tanuki

Under the scorching sun, a merchant could be seen tirelessly walking through the bustling markets. He had hoped to sell at least one of his wares. However, his stock was meager and rather outdated, so none seemed interested in what he had to offer. Days turned into weeks, and the merchant's fortunes failed to improve. Each evening, he returned home with unsold goods and a heart heavy with worry about own future.

One day, as he walked along the foot of a mountain, he felt more disheartened than ever. The path took him past a dense forest, where the sounds of nature seemed to echo his melancholy. Suddenly, a series of desperate squeals pierced the air. Curious, the merchant ventured into the woods, following the sound until he found a tanuki—a raccoon-like creature—trapped in a hunter's snare. Its hind leg was caught in the sharp, shiny claw trap, and it squirmed in pain.

With a kind heart and swift hands, the merchant used all his might to pry open the trap and free the tanuki. The creature, scared and panicked, quickly darted into the thick bushes and disappeared. The merchant, relieved that the tanuki was safe, continued on his way, a small sense of satisfaction easing his burden.

Days passed, and the merchant's luck remained unchanged. As he trudged along his usual path, he stumbled upon an old, rusty tea kettle lying abandoned on the ground. Though it was in poor condition, the merchant saw potential in it. He picked up the kettle, hoping he might sell it to the monks at the nearby Morin-ji Temple. He cleaned and polished the kettle until it gleamed almost like new. Hope glimmered in his eyes as he made his way to the temple.

To his delight, the monks at Morin-ji Temple needed a tea kettle for an upcoming service. The head monk inspected the kettle and, satisfied with its appearance, purchased it from the merchant. For the first time in many days, the merchant left with a big smile on his face, grateful for the much-needed fortune.

During the ceremony, the monks soon noticed something peculiar as they poured tea from the kettle. The tea cooled almost instantly, and they had to frequently reheat the kettle. The peculiar kettle also seemed to twitch and squirm in the pourer's hand when it was hot—as if it was alive. The head monk was unhappy, believing that he had been cheated by the merchant. And so, the following day, he summoned the merchant back to the temple to explain himself.

The innocent merchant arrived and examined the kettle. "I promise you, honorable monk, I sold you an ordinary kettle," he said earnestly. "There is nothing unusual about it."

Letting out a defeated sigh, the monk chose not to make the issue any more serious. He then invited the merchant for tea. So, the kettle was placed on the fire once more. Within moments, the metal began to sweat. Suddenly, it sprouted a scrubby tail, furry paws, and a pointed nose. With just a glance, the merchant immediately recognized the creature; it was in fact the tanuki that he had saved days before.

The kettle-turned-tanuki glanced at them with a sweet smile. "Thank you for freeing me," the tanuki said. "I wanted to repay your kindness by becoming a kettle you could sell. But being burned and polished was unbearable. I could not maintain my form."

The tea kettle tanuki.[28]

The monk and the merchant laughed, impressed by the tanuki's attempt at honor. They had both heard tales of shape-shifting tanuki who were known for their mischievous pranks. However, this tanuki's story was different—he genuinely wanted to help. From that day on, the tanuki became an esteemed guest at Morin-ji Temple. He entertained the monks with his tales and tricks, bringing joy to even the grumpiest among them. The merchant, too, often visited, sharing tea brewed in an ordinary kettle, grateful for the friendship of the magical creature.

The tale of the tanuki spread far and wide, attracting visitors to Morin-ji Temple. People flocked to see the famous shape-shifting tanuki and hear the story of his kindness and transformation. Morin-ji Temple, located in Gunma Prefecture, became renowned for not only its historical significance but also this enchanting legend. The story passed down through generations, a timeless reminder of the unexpected rewards of kindness and the magical possibilities that reside in the heart of Japanese folklore.

The Myth of Shuten Doji, the King of Oni

This next myth took place during the reign of Emperor Ichijo (the sixty-sixth emperor of Japan). At this time, the Japanese had been plagued with news of young women disappearing mysteriously. These women, often known for their beauty and purity, vanished without a trace. As the number of disappearances grew, the court sought the counsel of the imperial Onmyōdō.

After performing intricate rituals, the diviner revealed a chilling truth: the women were not simply missing but had been taken by a group of fearsome demons known as oni. These oni had established their stronghold on Mount Oe, where they reveled in their evil deeds. Oni in Japanese mythology are often depicted as large, fearsome creatures with sharp claws, wild hair, and horns protruding from their heads. They are notorious for their strength and malevolence, often causing chaos and destruction wherever they go.

Determined to put an end to the abductions, the imperial court summoned their most powerful warriors, led by Minamoto no Raiko, a renowned hero of his time.

Without hesitation, Raiko and his band of warriors embarked on a journey to eliminate the oni threat on Mount Oe. Before beginning their hunt, they visited three important shrines in the Kansai region to seek the blessings of the gods. Raiko himself visited Iwashimizu Hachimangū in Kyoto, the temple dedicated to Hachiman, the god of war and the patron deity of the popular Minamoto clan.

Understanding the danger of a direct assault on the oni, Raiko and his men chose to disguise themselves as yamabushi, ascetic monks or hermits who dwelled deep in the mountains. Yamabushi, practitioners of Shugendō, were respected for their spiritual prowess and lived harmoniously with nature and the supernatural. And so, dressed as monks, Raiko and his warriors made their way to Mount Oe, where they encountered three old men.

A statue of an oni in Japan.[29]

Without introducing themselves, the old men provided Raiko with valuable information about the oni's stronghold. They warned Raiko to be extremely cautious of the oni's leader, Shuten Doji, whose name literally means "Drunken Demon." Shuten Doji was the strongest and most fearsome of his kind, so defeating him would require divine intervention.

The old men then bestowed Raiko with a vial of magical sake and an unbreakable helmet. Raiko, looking at the items gifted by the mysterious old men, immediately knew that these wise men were not normal human beings but the deities that he and his men had prayed to previously. The warriors then bowed deeply, thanking the gods before continuing their mission.

As they approached the mountain, Raiko and his warriors encountered a young maiden by a river, washing a blood-stained cloth. The maiden, one of the oni's victims, revealed that the cloth belonged to another captive who had been devoured by the demons. Upon learning of the warriors' mission, she provided detailed directions to Shuten Doji's palace.

Upon reaching the palace, the warriors were almost immediately spotted by a group of oni. These monstrous demons were initially planning on devouring them whole. One oni, however, suggested that they present the strangers to Shuten Doji first, fearing their leader's wrath if they acted rashly. The disguised warriors were brought before the demon king, who expressed his surprise at their arrival.

"No human has ever found this place," Shuten Doji growled. "How did you get here?"

Raiko, seizing the opportunity, calmly responded, "We are followers of a great monk who once traveled these paths and laid down a way to your palace. Our teachings compel us to befriend demons."

Intrigued but still suspicious, Shuten Doji invited the warriors to stay the night. To test their sincerity, he offered them sake made from the blood of the noble maidens and a side of human flesh. Raiko and his men, though horrified, pretended to enjoy the offerings, explaining that their sect required them to accept any gifts from demons. Convinced by their act, Shuten Doji lowered his guard.

That night, Raiko saw his chance. He offered Shuten Doji and the others the magical sake gifted by the gods. To gain their trust, Raiko drank some first, knowing it was harmless to humans. Shuten Doji and his comrades, unable to resist, drank the sake eagerly. The enchanted drink rendered the demons impotent, causing them to pass out.

With the oni incapacitated, Raiko and his men shed their yamabushi disguises and unsheathed their weapons. They launched a fierce assault on the sleeping demons, slaying them one by one. Raiko, wearing the divine helmet, sneaked into Shuten Doji's chamber and aimed his blade at the demon king's throat. With a swift, clean slash, he severed Shuten Doji's head. However, the battle was not over. Shuten Doji's decapitated head, still clinging to the remainder of his life, flew toward Raiko in a desperate attempt to bite his head off. Thanks to the unbreakable helmet, Raiko was spared. The head finally fell lifeless, marking the end of the demon's reign of terror.

With Shuten Doji and his minions defeated, Raiko and his warriors freed the captive young women and led them back to Kyoto. In the city, they were celebrated as heroes. According to some sources, Raiko initially planned to bring Shuten Doji's severed head to the capital, but divine signs advised against bringing anything impure to the city, so he buried it instead.

Chapter 6 – Sea Whispers and River Songs

Water has always held a deep significance in Japanese culture, revered as a source of life and sustenance. Since ancient times, the Japanese have valued water not only for its life-giving properties but also for its spiritual and symbolic meanings. This deep respect is evident in various aspects of their daily lives, rituals, and, most vividly, their folklore.

In the earliest days of Japan, water was worshiped as a divine element. The country's numerous rivers, lakes, and oceans were seen as the abodes of gods and spirits. Agriculture, the primary livelihood for many, depended heavily on the regular flow of water. The practice of rice farming, which became central to Japanese society, is a clear reflection of the dependence on water. The careful irrigation systems designed to cultivate rice paddies showcase the meticulous relationship the Japanese maintained with water sources.

This reverence for water is also evident in the traditional occupation of ama, often referred to as the "Mermaids of Mie." These remarkable women, known for their free-diving skills, have harvested seafood, seaweed, and, most famously, pearls from the ocean's depths for over two thousand years. The ama divers' intimate connection with the sea embodies the deep respect and symbiotic relationship the Japanese people have with water. Their ability to dive without modern equipment—even oxygen tanks—and rely on breath control and endurance is a mark of human resilience and an acknowledgment of the ocean's mysterious and life-giving properties.

Ama divers, c. 1921.[30]

However, water's significance extends beyond being a source of life. In Japanese culture, water also serves as a bridge between worlds. Many Japanese myths and legends revolve around water bodies as gateways to other realms, places of mystery, and zones of peril. Rivers, lakes, and oceans are not just physical entities but are imbued with spiritual and supernatural dimensions.

This duality of water as both life-giver and gateway to the unknown is central to many aquatic myths. Water is a domain where benevolent spirits dwell, offering protection and blessings, but also where malevolent creatures lurk, posing dangers to the unwary. The Japanese people's intimate relationship with water is reflected in their folklore, which is full of tales of sea gods, dragon kings, and spirits inhabiting the waters. The first legend we are about to delve into is the most popular one: The Tale of Urashima Taro.

The Two Versions of Urashima Taro, the Man Who Visited the Dragon Palace

The story begins in a peaceful coastal village, far from the never-ending noise of the busy cities of Japan. Here lived a kind-hearted fisherman known as Urashima Taro. He was well-loved by the villagers for his gentle nature and his willingness to help others. Every day, Taro would set out in his small boat to fish in the sparkling blue sea, providing for his family and neighbors with the bounties he caught.

One sunny morning, as Taro was walking along the beach, he saw a group of children gathered around something. As he approached, he realized they were tormenting a small turtle, poking it with sticks and laughing at its attempts to escape. Taro's heart ached for the poor creature, and he quickly intervened.

Urashima Taro stopping the children from toying with the turtle.[31]

"Stop that!" he shouted, waving his arms to scare the children away. "How can you be so cruel to this innocent turtle?" The children, startled by Taro's stern voice, scattered and ran off. Gently, Taro picked up the turtle, noticing its trembling body and frightened eyes.

"Don't worry, little one," he said softly. "You're safe now." He carried the turtle to the edge of the water and set it down gently on the sand. The turtle looked up at him, as if to say thank you, and slowly made its way back into the sea. Perhaps content with seeing the small turtle saved and free from harm, Urashima Taro smiled and went about his day as usual.

The very next day, Taro went fishing from his boat. Suddenly, he noticed a turtle swimming in his direction. He immediately recognized the creature: it was the same turtle he had saved yesterday. However, much to his astonishment, the turtle began to speak.

"Kind fisherman, I am the turtle you saved yesterday," it said. "I am grateful for your kindness and wish to repay you. Please, come with me to the Dragon Palace beneath the sea, where the beautiful Princess Otohime wishes to thank you personally."

Though surprised, Taro felt a sense of adventure and agreed. After giving the fisherman a set of gills, the turtle instructed him to climb onto its back. Then, with a magical swirl, they dove beneath the waves. Taro marveled at the underwater world around him, filled with coral reefs, schools of fish, and fantastical sea creatures.

Soon, they arrived at the Dragon Palace, a magnificent structure made of coral and pearls, glowing with an ethereal light. Taro was led inside, where he was greeted by Princess Otohime, the most beautiful woman he had ever seen. Her hair flowed like ebony, and her eyes sparkled like the great ocean.

"Welcome, Urashima Taro," she said with a warm smile. "Thank you for saving the turtle. Please, stay with us and enjoy the wonders of our palace."

Taro was treated to a grand feast, with the most delicious food and drink he had ever tasted. He was entertained by graceful dancers and enchanting music, and for what felt like days, he experienced the joys of the Dragon Palace. Princess Otohime spent much time with him, and Taro found himself falling in love with her gentle nature and beauty. However, despite the paradise around him, Taro began to miss his family and village. He approached Princess Otohime and expressed his desire to return home.

"I understand," she said, her eyes filled with sadness. "But before you leave, I wish to give you a gift." She handed him a beautiful lacquered box tied with a silk cord. "This is the tamatebako, a little something to remember me by. Keep it close to you, but please, do not open it."

Then, with a heavy heart, Taro thanked the princess and climbed onto the back of the turtle, who swiftly carried him back to shore. Taro stepped onto the same beach where he had saved the turtle, but something felt different. The village in which he had lived his entire life seemed altered, and the people were unfamiliar. After asking some strangers what had happened to his dear village, Taro soon realized that many years had passed since he had left—a few centuries, at the very least. His family and friends were long gone, and everything he had known had changed.

Distraught and confused, Taro remembered the tamatebako. Believing it might hold the answer to his predicament, he untied the silk cord and opened the box. As he did, a thick cloud of white smoke enveloped him, and he suddenly felt weak and tired. His hair turned white, and wrinkles appeared on his skin. When the smoke cleared, Taro found that he had aged rapidly, becoming an old man in an instant.

Urashima Taro turning old after opening the tamatebako.[32]

As it turned out, the magic of the Dragon Palace had kept him young, but once the box was opened, time caught up with him. Only now did he remember Princess Otohime's warning to not open the box, but it was too late. With a mixture of sorrow and acceptance, Taro sat by the shore, gazing out at the vast ocean. While his dream of an adventure had come true, he had also lost so much.

The legend of Urashima Taro is a folktale that points to the passage of time and the fleeting nature of life, urging us to cherish each moment and the people we love. However, there is an older version of the tale, recorded in the Otogi Bunko during the Muromachi period, that focuses more on the theme of love.

In this version, Urashima Taro is not just a kind-hearted fisherman but a young man who falls deeply in love with Otohime, the beautiful daughter of the Dragon King of the Sea. The story begins with Taro setting out to fish one morning. As he casts his line, he feels a strong tug and reels in a magnificent turtle. Amazed by its size and beauty, Taro contemplates his catch but ultimately decides to release it back into the ocean, showing compassion and respect for the creature.

The next day, when Taro went fishing again, he encountered a beautiful woman who claimed to be the turtle he had saved. Expressing her gratitude, and perhaps attracted to the kind-hearted man, she proposed they get married and invited Taro to come with her.

"Close your eyes," she said to the fisherman.

Urashima Taro and the princess.[33]

A few moments later, Taro opened his eyes to see that they were nearing the legendary island of Mount Horai—the fabled mountain where the Chinese Emperor Qin Shi Huang once believed the elixir of life to be hidden. There, Taro realized that the woman was a princess known as Kamehime. From there, the princess took Taro to see her parents before throwing a ceremony in which they were wed.

From that point on, the story closely follows the modern version. Taro enjoyed a life of luxury with his wife for three years until he eventually grew homesick. As the feeling of missing home grew stronger, he decided to go home just for a little while to visit his parents. Princess Kamehime was angry at first. "How can you stand a day without my presence when I can't even live a second without seeing you?"

However, knowing that nothing could stop her husband, she relented. She gave Taro a jeweled comb box. "I hope you won't forget about me, and should you ever want to come back, hold this box tight. But remember to never open it."

The ending of this version, however, is the same. Engulfed in sadness as soon as he learned that three hundred years had passed and his once familiar village was but a thing of the past, Taro wandered through the village, mourning the loss of everything and everyone he had once known. In his despair, Taro clutched the jeweled comb box Otohime had given him. He thought of her and how much he missed her. Overcome by his longing to see her again, he forgot his promise and decided to open the box.

Taro aged rapidly, his youth fading in an instant. Realizing his mistake, he understood that he would never see his beloved Otohime again. The box, meant to symbolize their eternal bond, had become the instrument of their final separation.

Kappa, a Turtle-Like Creature in Rivers

The origins of the kappa are as murky as the rivers they inhabit. Some believe the first mention of a kappa dates to a text from the eighth century, which described a "river deity." This suggests that kappa have been part of Japan's spiritual world for over a millennium. Another theory, however, is much darker. In ancient times, it was said that families who could not care for their stillborn babies, often due to poverty or disability, would cast them into the river. These abandoned souls were thought to transform into kappa, forever haunting the waters where they were discarded.

A depiction of kappa.[34]

Rivers, ponds, and lakes are kappa playgrounds, hunting grounds, and homes. Physically, kappa are about the size of a small child, but their appearance is anything but innocent. They have scaly—and at times, hairy—reptilian skin, webbed hands and feet, a beak as their mouth, and a shell-like carapace on their backs. Their most distinctive feature, however, is the hollow indentation on top of their heads, which holds water. If the water spills or dries out, the kappa becomes weak and powerless, almost unable to move until the cavity is refilled with water from its home.

Despite their vulnerability, kappa are known for their mischievous and often malevolent behavior. They lurk near water, waiting to pounce on unsuspecting victims. Their pranks can range from harmless—like peeking under women's kimonos—to deadly, such as drowning people and animals, kidnapping children, and even consuming human flesh. Kappa also have a reputation for tormenting animals, especially horses and cows. In one story, a kappa was caught stealing horses and was forced to write a vow never to harm humans again.

Kappa have a peculiar obsession with politeness. If you bow to a kappa, it feels compelled to return the gesture. This quirk has been used to outsmart them, as seen in the tale of a sumo wrestler who was challenged by a kappa. Knowing the kappa's weakness, the wrestler accepted its challenge to a sumo match. In sumo wrestling, it is customary to bow to your opponent at the beginning of a match, showing respect and acknowledging the forthcoming contest. And so, as they prepared to grapple, the wrestler performed a deep bow. The kappa, driven by its compulsion for politeness, instinctively returned the bow, causing the water in its head to spill out. Instantly weakened, the kappa lost its strength, allowing the wrestler to easily overpower and defeat it.

Kappa also have detachable arms, and if an arm is pulled off, the kappa will often perform favors or reveal valuable secrets to get it back. This characteristic highlights their paradoxical nature—powerful yet easily subdued by those who understand their quirks. Moreover, kappa have a strong dislike for iron. They become agitated when iron objects fall into the water and can be repelled by those carrying iron. Some tales recount kappa offering rewards to anyone who helps remove iron objects from their watery habitat. This peculiar combination of physical vulnerabilities and specific dislikes adds depth to the kappa's character, making them both fearsome and approachable entities, depending on one's knowledge and approach.

Interestingly, kappa have a particular fondness for cucumbers, which are often used to appease them. In ancient Tokyo, families would write their names on cucumbers and float them downriver to keep kappa at bay. Some even believed that eating cucumbers before swimming would protect them from kappa attacks, though opinions on this practice varied.

Despite their menacing reputation, kappa are not entirely malevolent. If treated kindly, a kappa can become a loyal ally. They might help farmers irrigate their fields or bring fresh fish as a gift, which is considered a sign of good fortune. Kappa are also said to possess great knowledge of medicine. According to legends, kappa were skilled in the art of treating broken bones and dislocated joints. They were said to have a deep understanding of human anatomy and the ability to realign bones with remarkable precision. Some even believe that the kappa were the ones who taught these skills to early practitioners of traditional Japanese medicine. This knowledge of bone setting, now known as sekkotsu, became an integral part of Japanese medical practices, particularly among village healers and those specializing in martial arts injuries.

Due to their complex nature, kappa are sometimes venerated as water deities. Shrines dedicated to kappa can be found in various regions, including Aomori and Miyagi Prefectures. Festivals aimed at appeasing kappa and ensuring a bountiful harvest continue to this day, reflecting their enduring significance in Japanese culture.

The Tale of Hoori and Toyotama-hime

In ancient times, when the land and sea worlds were closer than they are today, there lived a young hunter named Hoori. One day, Hoori lost his older brother Hoderi's precious fishhook while fishing. Desperate to find it, he decided to visit Ryūgū, the majestic underwater palace of the sea god, hoping to seek permission to search its grounds.

As Hoori wandered through the enchanting gardens of Ryūgū, he came across a beautiful woman by a well. This was Toyotama-hime, the daughter of the sea god. Their eyes met, and they found each other so captivating that they quickly fell in love and were soon married.

For three years, Hoori lived blissfully with Toyotama-hime in the underwater palace, but as time passed, he remembered his quest to find the lost fishhook. His longing for the hook grew, and he became increasingly despondent. Seeing her husband's sorrow, Toyotama-hime confided in her father about Hoori's plight.

The sea god then summoned Hoori and asked, "What troubles you, my son?"

"I have lost my brother's fishhook, and I cannot return without it," Hoori replied sadly.

Determined to help, the sea god called upon all the fish in the ocean. "Has any of you seen a lost fishhook?" he asked. A large tai fish immediately swam forward and confessed, "There is something lodged in my throat that has caused me great pain." When the sea god inspected it, he found Hoori's missing hook.

The sea god handed the fishhook to Hoori. "Here is what you seek. Take it and return to your world. But know this: I will also bless your fields with rain and prosperity while denying it to your brother."

The sea god gave Hoori two magical jewels, the tide-controlling manju and kanju. "These will protect you from your brother's wrath," he said. With that, the sea god set Hoori on the back of an enormous dragon, who carried him swiftly back to the surface world.

True to the sea god's word, Hoori's fields flourished, while Hoderi's harvests withered. Furious and envious, Hoderi attacked Hoori, but Hoori raised the tide with the magical jewels, drowning his brother. Only when Hoderi swore eternal submission did Hoori lower the tide, sparing his life.

During this time, Toyotama-hime became pregnant with Hoori's child. When her time came, she and her sister Tamayori-hime traveled to the surface on the back of a giant turtle. "Hoori, please build me a birthing hut thatched with cormorant feathers by the shore," she asked.

Hoori hastened to build the hut, but Toyotama-hime went into labor before it was completed. She entered the unfinished hut and turned to Hoori. "To give birth, I must return to my natural form. Promise me you will not look upon me," she pleaded.

Unsurprisingly, Hoori's curiosity got the better of him. Unable to resist, he peeked inside the hut and saw Toyotama-hime in her true form—an enormous wani, a sea dragon, writhing and creeping about.

Ashamed and heartbroken that her true form had been seen, Toyotama-hime decided she could no longer stay in the land of humans. Despite her love for Hoori, she returned to the sea, leaving their newborn son behind. Before she left, she closed the path between the land and sea, forever separating their worlds.

Toyotama-hime felt betrayed, yet her love for Hoori remained. And so, she asked her sister, Tamayori-hime, to care for the child. "Take care of him for me," she said, her voice tinged with sorrow.

Tamayori-hime raised the boy, who was named Ugayafukiaezu. When he grew up, he married Tamayori-hime, and together they had four children. One of their sons would become the legendary Emperor Jimmu, the first emperor of Japan, symbolizing the lasting bond between the worlds of land and sea.

The stories of Urashima Taro, the kappa, and Hoori and Toyotama-hime are full of lessons about respecting nature, the dangers of greed, and the virtues of compassion and bravery. Urashima Taro's journey reminds us that life is fleeting and that we should cherish the world around us. The kappa, with its mix of mischief and danger, shows that understanding and respecting nature can lead to harmony. The tale of Hoori and Toyotama-hime highlights how all living things are connected and the importance of respecting the mysteries of nature.

These stories also caution against greed. Urashima Taro's curiosity, which leads him to open the tamatebako and age instantly, serves as a warning against temptation. Hoori's use of the tide-controlling jewels to the point that he was willing to drown his brother, illustrates the destructive potential of greed. However, amidst these warnings, there are also stories of kindness and bravery. Urashima Taro's act of kindness earns him a magical journey, while the kappa can become a helpful ally when treated with respect. Hoori's brave journey and his love for Toyotama-hime also reflect the courage required to bridge different worlds.

These tales reflect how deeply Japanese culture reveres water. As an island nation, Japan's history, culture, and daily life are closely tied to the sea, rivers, and lakes. These stories remind us to maintain harmony with nature, live with compassion and bravery, and respect the waters that give us life.

Chapter 7 – Adventures and Legends in the Wild

Two men, weary and lost, trudged through the dense forest as night descended. As the air grew colder and the sounds of the forest grew more eerie, the men's desperation for shelter intensified. They stumbled upon a small hut.

Knocking on the door, they were greeted by an old woman, her gnarled hands busy spinning thread.

"Please, good lady, may we shelter here for the night?" one of the men asked, his voice trembling.

The old woman squinted at them. "My hut is small and modest," she said. "It is not fit for men dressed as fine as yourselves."

"We beg of you," the other man implored. "The woods are dangerous, and we fear for our lives. We ask for nothing more than a corner to rest until dawn."

The old woman sighed, a deep, resigned sound. "Very well,' she said reluctantly. "But promise me one thing. Do not, under any circumstances, open the door to the inner room."

"You have our words," the men chorused, relief flooding their faces.

As the hours passed, the old woman went out, leaving the men alone in the dimly lit hut. Curiosity gnawed at them. What could be so precious that the old woman guarded it so fiercely? They exchanged furtive glances. Unable to resist, tiptoed to the forbidden door. Quietly, they opened it a crack and peered inside.

Their faces blanched with horror. Piles of bodies and ancient bones lay heaped in the room, the grisly remains of those who had come before them. The men quickly shut the door, their hearts pounding with fear. They gathered their belongings, but as they moved toward the door, they heard the old woman returning. She sensed their betrayal immediately. Her form began to change: horns sprouted from her forehead, and her fangs gleamed under the moonlight. The legendary Yamamba, the mountain witch, stood before them.

A depiction of Yamamba (also spelled Yama-uba).[35]

"You broke your promise," she snarled, her voice a guttural growl.

Terrified, the men bolted from the hut, running as fast as their legs could carry them. They recited sutras, hoping the benevolent power of the Buddha would protect them. Yamamba pursued them, her rage palpable, but the men's prayers seemed to slow her down.

As they neared the edge of the village, the witch was forced to retreat. The sacred ground of the village was beyond her reach, and she melted back into the shadows of the mountains.

Breathing heavily, the men collapsed at the village's edge, safe at last. They had narrowly escaped the witch's wrath.

Yamamba's nature was rather complex. She was neither purely evil nor kind. While she killed those who broke their promises, she was also known to help humans—like many other mythical creatures of Japanese beliefs. Farmers and weavers spoke of her assistance in their labor, a mysterious force that sometimes worked in their favor.

This tale, like many others, reveals Japan's untamed mountains, forests, and rural areas. These wild places were full of surprises, harboring spirits and supernatural beings that guarded or haunted the grounds. Some people avoided venturing too deep into the unknown, while others sought the thrill of adventure. Mothers would warn their children to steer clear of these places, and should they ever get lost in forests or the wild, to always respect their surroundings lest they anger the spirits (kami) dwelling within.

Another tale of the untamed written in the eleventh century provides a more heartwarming story. It begins in a small village called Kamiide, believed to be in the Suruga Province. The story centers around a young boy named Yosoji. His village had been plagued by a devastating smallpox epidemic, and among the afflicted was his mother. Her condition grew worse each day, and Yosoji's heart ached as he watched her suffer.

Desperate to find a cure, Yosoji sought out a fortune teller, hoping for a miracle. The old seer listened to his plight and, after a moment of deep thought, spoke. "There is a stream at the foot of Mount Fuji," he said. "Its waters have the power to cure disease. Bring this water to your mother, and she will recover."

Filled with hope, Yosoji set out on his journey the very next day. As he ventured into the woods, he came across three different paths. Each seemed equally likely, but he had no idea which one to take. The description given by the fortune teller had been vague, leaving Yosoji confused.

Just then, a young girl dressed in white emerged from the bushes and approached him. "Are you lost?" she asked, her voice gentle and soothing.

Yosoji, though puzzled by her sudden appearance, felt a glimmer of hope. "I need to find a stream at the foot of Mount Fuji," he explained. "It's for my mother; she's very ill."

The girl smiled softly. "Follow me," she said. "I know the way."

Yosoji followed her, and soon they arrived at the small stream the fortune teller had spoken of. The girl stood by as Yosoji carefully scooped some water into a flask. "Thank you," he said, his heart swelling with gratitude.

He hurried back to his village and gave the water to his mother. Days passed, and her condition began to improve. Yosoji's joy was boundless, but he knew his task was not yet complete. He returned to the forest, hoping to find the girl again.

At the crossroads of the three paths, he saw her once more. She greeted him with a serene smile. "Return here in three days," she instructed. "You must make five trips to the stream to cure the entire village."

Yosoji nodded and followed her instructions faithfully. On each trip, he collected more water, and each time, the villagers' health improved. By the end of the fifth journey, the smallpox epidemic had been vanquished, and the village was filled with celebration. The villagers thanked Yosoji for his bravery and determination.

The spirit showing Yosoji the stream.[36]

Knowing he owed his success to the girl in white, Yosoji went back to the forest, hoping to see her one last time. But when he arrived at the stream, he found it dried up, and the girl was nowhere to be seen. He knelt by the dry bed and prayed, asking for her to reveal herself so he could express his gratitude.

As if in answer to his prayers, the girl appeared. Yosoji's heart leaped with joy. "Thank you for everything," he said earnestly. "May I know your name so I can tell the villagers who our true savior is?"

The girl smiled, a mysterious glint in her eyes. "My name is not important," she replied gently. "Farewell, Yosoji."

With that, she swung a branch of camellia over her head. A magical scene unfolded before Yosoji's eyes: a cloud descended from Mount Fuji and enveloped her. The cloud lifted her into the sky, revealing her true identity. She was none other than Konohanasakuya-hime, the goddess of Mount Fuji.

Yosoji watched in awe as she ascended, her divine presence illuminating the night. He returned to the village, carrying the tale of their miraculous savior, forever grateful for the goddess's kindness.

Not all tales of the untamed were told to instill fear. This legend of Mount Fuji and the benevolent kami Konohanasakuya-hime exemplifies the wonders and surprises that nature holds.

The Tragic Legend of Yamato Takeru

From the early days of his youth, Prince Ousu, later known as Yamato Takeru, had been surrounded by a sense of destiny. As the youngest son of Emperor Keikō and the elder lady of Inabi, he was raised in the shadow of the Yamato clan's divine lineage, said to be descended from the sun goddess Amaterasu.

One fateful day, Prince Ousu committed an act that would forever alter his life. In a fit of rage or perhaps a twisted sense of justice, he killed his brother. This act of fratricide cast a dark shadow over his character and instilled a deep-seated fear in his father. Emperor Keikō, believing that his son harbored a dangerous and malevolent nature, chose not to punish him directly but sent him away on a dangerous mission.

"Go to the land of the Kumaso," the emperor decreed, his voice cold and unyielding. "Quell their rebellion or perish in the attempt."

The Kumaso people were fierce warriors who refused to submit to the central rule of the Yamato clan. Their chiefs were feared for their strength and brutality. It was a mission that seemed almost certain to fail, a task designed to rid the emperor of his troublesome son. Undeterred, Prince Ousu accepted the challenge, determined to prove his worth.

Before setting out, he journeyed to the sacred Ise Shrine to seek the blessing of Amaterasu. There, he met his aunt, the high priestess of the Ise Shrine. She saw the turmoil in his eyes and the burden he carried. "Take this robe," she said, handing him an exquisite silk garment. "It will bring you luck and protect you on your journey."

With his wife, Princess Ototachibana, and a few loyal followers, Prince Ousu set out to confront the Kumaso. His journey was dangerous, but his cunning and bravery soon earned him a new name. He learned that the Kumaso were having a feast, and this was indeed a golden opportunity for the young prince to strike. Attacking head-on, however, was suicide. So, he planned to sneak into the banquet. Donning the robe his aunt had gifted him, the prince disguised himself as a female servant. He let down his hair, styled it with a comb, and adorned it with jewelry. His soft features made it easy to pass as a female servant. The prince entered the banquet without suspicion. The leader of the Kumaso is said to have called the disguised prince, demanding he pour wine faster, to which he gladly obliged. He was, after all, waiting for his enemies to get drunk.

Then, the moment the Kumaso were thoroughly drunk, the prince made his move. He unsheathed a small knife concealed beneath his robe and swiftly attacked the Kumaso chief. This daring feat earned him the name Yamato Takeru, which simply means "The Brave of Yamato." After quelling the rebellion just as his father had instructed, Yamato Takeru made his way home. On his way, the prince added more feats to his list of achievements, slaying several divine beings believed to be hostile to the Yamato rule.

A depiction of Yamato Takeru battling a certain sea monster.[37]

However, despite his victory, Emperor Keikō remained unmoved. He viewed his son with the same suspicion and fear as before. "Go to the eastern lands and obliterate those who refuse to submit to my rule," he commanded, sending Yamato Takeru on yet another perilous mission.

At this, Takeru revealed his more vulnerable human side. The prince, aware of his father's intentions, confided in his aunt. "I know my father wishes for my demise," he said, his voice heavy with sorrow.

His aunt, touched by his plight, gave him the legendary sword Kusanagi. "This sword," she said, "was found in the tail of the great serpent slain by Susanoo, the great kami of storms. It will protect you as you face your destiny."

Yamato Takeru set out once more, accompanied by his faithful wife. However, their voyage was treacherous. As they crossed the sea, a violent storm threatened to capsize their vessel. Princess Ototachibana sacrificed herself to the god of the sea, soothing the divine being's anger and allowing her husband to continue his quest. Grieving but resolute, Yamato Takeru pressed on, conquering foes both mortal and divine.

His path led him to Ashigara Pass, where he encountered a deity in the form of a deer. Seeing through the disguise, he slew the deity, making the passage safe for future travelers. He also successfully subdued a deity in Shinano (modern-day Gunma Prefecture) before reaching Owari. It was also here that he married Princess Miyazu, finding a brief respite in his arduous journey.

Yamato Takeru's final challenge came at Mount Ibuki, a sacred mountain shrouded in legend. Confident in his strength, he left the Kusanagi sword behind and set out to confront the mountain deity barehanded. On his ascent, he encountered a large white boar—or according to some sources, a white snake—which he believed was the deity's messenger. Respecting the creature, he did not kill it, unaware that it was the deity itself.

The deity, enraged by the prince's blasphemy, conjured a powerful hailstorm. The icy winds howled through the mountains, battering Yamato Takeru with relentless force. Hailstones the size of fists pelted him, and the once clear path turned into a treacherous, frozen maze. Disoriented and exhausted, the brave prince staggered through the storm. The deity's curse seeped into his bones, sapping his vitality and leaving him feverish and weak.

He struggled to find his way and fortunately stumbled upon a spring at Samegai. He drank deeply, the refreshing liquid offering a momentary reprieve from his torment. For a brief period, the prince felt his former strength returning, but the respite was fleeting. The curse of the mountain deity was too potent. He knew his end was near.

Yamato Takeru and the sword Kusanagi.[38]

With his last breath, he gazed up at the sky, a profound peace washing over him. His spirit, unshackled from his mortal form, transformed into a majestic white bird. The bird took flight, soaring through the heavens, its pure form gliding gracefully back to his kin.

When the white bird reached the imperial palace, Emperor Keikō saw the spirit of his son. At that moment, the emperor's heart softened, and he finally understood the true worth and unparalleled bravery of Yamato Takeru. The fear and suspicion that had clouded his judgment lifted, replaced by a deep sense of loss and regret. To honor the valiant prince who had fought so bravely for the Yamato Kingdom, he erected a grand mausoleum, a lasting tribute to Yamato Takeru's courage and sacrifice.

Tengu, the Spirits of the Mountains

Tengu are one of the most enigmatic and formidable creatures in Japanese folklore. Often depicted as mountain goblins or warrior spirits, these supernatural beings are both revered and feared. They are typically portrayed with a combination of human and avian features: red-faced with sharp, piercing eyes and sometimes wings and the beak of a bird. As time passed, the depiction of tengu evolved, and they became more anthropomorphic. Sometimes they were shown with a long, prominent nose rather than a beak, hinting at their transformation from avian spirits to human-like warriors.

Tengu masks.[39]

Tengu are known for their martial prowess, often depicted as skilled swordsmen and masters of disguise. They are closely associated with yamabushi, or mountain ascetic monks, and frequently take on their appearance. These monks, who practiced a form of Shugendō—a belief system combining Shinto, Buddhism, and Taoism—were known for their rigorous training and mystical practices in the mountains.

One legend involving tengu begins with the Empress Dowager Fujiwara no Akirakeiko, also known as the Somedono Empress, the mother of Emperor Seiwa. The empress was constantly afflicted by a spiritual ailment, frequently suffering from spirit possessions. Many prayers and rituals were conducted for her recovery, and numerous monks and priests were summoned to perform these rites, yet the empress remained tormented.

In search of a solution, the court heard of a monk living in a remote temple atop Mount Katsuragi in what is now Nara Prefecture. This monk had honed his magical rituals over many years and possessed extraordinary powers. It was said he could send his bowl flying to fetch food and his bottle to retrieve water, all without moving a muscle. Intrigued by these tales of his abilities, the emperor dispatched envoys to summon this monk to the palace, hoping he could cure the empress.

The monk agreed to help and commenced a ritual to expel the malicious spirit plaguing the empress. During the ritual, one of the empress's servants suddenly began to cry and laugh uncontrollably. She was restrained and beaten as the monk chanted his incantations. A fox then sprang out from her clothing, revealing itself to be a kitsune—the spirit responsible for haunting the empress. With additional rituals, the monk successfully dispersed the kitsune, and the empress began to recover.

Grateful for the monk's success, the emperor invited him to stay at the imperial palace. The monk enjoyed the comforts and luxuries of the palace, but his stay took a dark turn. One day, he glimpsed the empress in her private chambers, clad only in her undergarments. Consumed by desire and perhaps influenced by evil whispers, the monk attempted to assault her. The empress's cries alerted her ladies-in-waiting, who quickly summoned Taima no Kamotsugu, the court physician. Kamotsugu apprehended the monk and brought him before the emperor.

Furious and betrayed, the emperor had the monk imprisoned. The monk, however, did not regret his action. Instead, he declared his desire to see the empress again and vowed to become a demon after death if necessary. His sinister vow was reported to the emperor, who then ordered the monk's exile to the mountains.

In his mountain exile, the monk's obsession festered. Desperate to reunite with the empress, he starved himself to death, fully intent on transforming into a demon. His malevolent wish was granted, and he became a tengu. He turned into a figure eight feet tall with a bald head, skin as black as a crow, and eyes that gleamed with malice. Wielding a magical hammer and wearing only a loincloth, he descended upon the imperial palace, striking fear into the hearts of all who beheld him.

The tengu infiltrated the empress's bedchamber and possessed her, spending nights with her while she was entranced. Each morning, the maids found her with no memory of the encounters. Alarmed, they reported these events to the emperor. The emperor, more concerned for the empress's future than frightened by the tengu, ordered further rituals to banish the demon. The tengu also sought revenge against

Kamotsugu, whose fear led to his untimely death, followed by the mysterious deaths of his sons.

For a time, the rituals succeeded, and the empress's condition improved. However, the respite was short-lived. The tengu soon returned to the empress's bedchamber, resuming his nightly visits. The story ends on a cliffhanger, leaving the fate of the empress and the tengu unresolved. The moral of the tale, as recounted by old storytellers, was a warning that noblewomen should avoid relationships with priests, as such liaisons could lead to disaster.

However, not all stories about tengu revolve around the creature being a malice to human beings.

The phenomenon of people disappearing mysteriously (generally known as kamikakushi) was often attributed to the handiwork of kami or other divine spirits, and tengu were frequently implicated. This mysterious abduction done specifically by a tengu is known as tengu sarai. Tengu were said to snatch people away, especially children, and take them to the mountains. These children often returned with fear and trauma, but in rare cases, they came back profoundly changed.

One of the most famous examples of a tengu abduction was a seven-year-old boy from the Edo period named Torakichi. His experience was meticulously documented by a Shinto scholar, Hirata Atsutane. According to the records, Torakichi was spirited away by tengu and spent five years with them. During this time, he traveled to different otherworldly places, saw the moon up close, and acquired many skills. He learned martial arts, medicine, calligraphy, and weapon-making under the guidance of the tengu. Upon his return, Torakichi exhibited extraordinary abilities and knowledge far beyond his years.

While they are often feared for their mischievous and sometimes malevolent actions, tengu also possess great wisdom and mastery of martial arts. This duality is reflected in the belief held by some that tengu are the reincarnated spirits of Buddhist priests who were proud and self-important in life. This notion explains why tengu frequently take the form of yamabushi, or mountain ascetic monks, as a reflection of their past lives and their connection to spiritual and martial disciplines.

Tengu have a reputation for being exceptional swordsmen. They also tend to mentor those they deem worthy in the skills of martial arts. This mentorship often involves rigorous training and the imparting of secret techniques that are otherwise inaccessible to ordinary humans. One of the most renowned examples of a tengu mentor is Sōjōbō, the king of the tengu, who is said to reside on Mount Kurama.

Minamoto no Yoshitsune, one of Japan's most celebrated warriors, is famously associated with Sōjōbō and the tengu. According to legend, Yoshitsune was sent to a temple on Mount Kurama after his father's demise in a war. There, he was trained by the king of the tengu.

Minamoto no Yoshitsune training under the tutelage of Sōjōbō.[40]

Under Sōjōbō's tutelage, Yoshitsune mastered the art of the sword, learning techniques that enabled him to move with extraordinary speed and agility. He also gained insights into military strategy and the use of magic in combat. These skills proved invaluable during the Genpei War, where Yoshitsune led the Minamoto clan to victory against the Taira clan, securing his place in Japanese history as a legendary warrior.

Chapter 8 – Ghost Tales

The story of Okiku has many different variations, but the most popular one begins at Himeji Castle, where the legend is believed to have originated. Okiku was a servant at the castle, responsible for washing dishes. When she first entered the castle's service, she marveled at the many treasures it held, but none were as precious as the ten exquisite plates used by the lord to entertain high-ranking guests. Okiku knew she had to handle these plates with utmost care, for even a single chip could mean her death.

Okiku's beauty was renowned throughout the castle, attracting the attention of many, particularly the samurai retainers. Among them, one samurai named Aoyama became infatuated with her. His desire for Okiku grew so intense that he would do anything to have her.

One day, Aoyama approached her. "Okiku," he said, his eyes intense with longing, "I cannot hide my feelings any longer. I wish to marry you."

Okiku's heart pounded in her chest. She bowed respectfully and replied, "My lord, I am honored, but I do not share your feelings."

Aoyama's face darkened with disappointment. "You will come to love me in time," he insisted, but Okiku remained firm in her refusal.

Days turned into weeks, and Aoyama's frustration grew. He tried to woo her with gifts and kind words, but nothing swayed her. Finally, in a fit of desperation, he devised a sinister plan to force her into submission.

One evening, after the castle had quieted down, Aoyama crept into the room where the treasured plates were kept. With a sly grin, he took one of the ten plates and hid it. The next day, he confronted Okiku, his tone accusatory.

"One of the plates is missing," he said, his voice cold and threatening. "Do you know what this means?"

Okiku's eyes widened in horror. She rushed to count the plates, her hands trembling. "One, two, three, four, five, six, seven, eight, nine," she whispered, her heart sinking. She counted again and again, but there were only nine.

"Please, Aoyama. I swear I did not lose the plate!" she cried, tears streaming down her face.

Aoyama feigned concern, but his eyes gleamed with malice. "Okiku," he said softly, "I can tell the lord it wasn't your fault. But you must agree to be mine."

Despite her fear, Okiku stood her ground. "No, my lord. I cannot."

Her refusal ignited Aoyama's fury. He grabbed her roughly and beat her with a wooden sword. Okiku cried out in pain, but she did not relent. Enraged, Aoyama tied her and suspended her over a well in the courtyard.

"You will change your mind," he snarled, dunking her into the cold, dark water, "or you will die."

Each time he pulled her up, gasping for air, he demanded her compliance. Each time, she refused. Finally, in a fit of blind rage, Aoyama drew his katana and struck her down, her lifeless body falling into the well.

In Japanese folklore, spirits are believed to pass on to the afterlife unless held back by strong emotions. A person who dies unjustly may become an onryō, a vengeful spirit, driven by the need for retribution. Unlike yokai, which are supernatural creatures, yūrei are spirits of the dead (ghosts), and onryō are among the most feared, capable of causing great harm.

After her death, Okiku transformed into an onryō. One night, her mutilated form arose from the well to walk the castle halls, searching for the missing plate. "One, two, three, four, five, six, seven, eight, nine," she would count, her voice echoing through the halls. Then, a heart-wrenching scream would follow, chilling anyone who heard it. Those who heard part of her counting fell ill, while those who heard the full count died of fright. Aoyama, tormented by her nightly visits, was driven mad by lack of sleep.

The castle's lord, desperate to end the haunting, called upon a priest to cleanse the grounds. The priest, wise and cunning, awaited Okiku's nightly appearance. When she reached nine in her count, he quickly shouted, "Ten!" Okiku's spirit, seemingly satisfied that the missing plate was found, finally found peace. Her tormented expression softened, and she disappeared into the well, never to return again.

Yet, some say Okiku's spirit did not rest entirely. In 1795, a strange infestation of caterpillars plagued Japan's wells. These insects, resembling a tied-up woman, were believed to be Okiku's lingering spirit. The caterpillar became known as Okiku mushi. Today, this insect is commonly known as the jakō ageha, or the Chinese windmill (Byasa alcinous), a haunting reminder of her tragic fate.

Okiku's story became so famous that it has been adapted into various forms of media over the centuries. Her tale has inspired plays, books, and movies, capturing the imagination of audiences worldwide. Her story inspired the popular horror movie *The Ring*, known as *Ringu* in Japan. The film features a vengeful spirit with a similar tragic backstory, highlighting how deeply ingrained Okiku's legend is in Japanese culture and how it continues to inspire modern interpretations of ghost stories.

Indeed, Japan's rich folklore is home to countless ghost stories, but three stand out as the most famous and influential. They are known as Nihon san dai kaidan or Japan's Big Three Ghost Stories. Okiku's story is one of the three, and the second we are about to explore also revolves around revenge. Today, it remains one of the most chilling and compelling ghost stories in Japanese history.

Oiwa's Curse

The story takes place in the Edo period and follows a kind-hearted woman named Oiwa. She was married to Tamiya Iemon, a ronin. Unlike the legendary samurai of the past, Iemon was a wasteful man and a thief, notorious for his misdeeds. For the longest time, the couple did not live a happy married life; their days were often filled with Iemon throwing a fit and Oiwa absorbing his anger, hoping one day he would change for the better. That was, however, until one day when Oiwa sensed that Iemon would never improve himself. She made up her mind to finally leave him. Oiwa confided in her father, who was also a ronin at the time. And so, after listening to his daughter's laments, Oiwa's father confronted Iemon and demanded that he divorce Oiwa. He also knew that Iemon had lived a life far from the honorable path.

"You have disgraced our family enough, Iemon," he declared, his voice firm with authority. "Leave my daughter and never return."

Enraged by his father-in-law's ultimatum and fearing the exposure of his crimes, Iemon drew his sword and murdered Iowa's father in cold blood. Returning home, he lied to Oiwa, claiming that her father had been killed by bandits on the road. He begged her to reconcile with him, promising to avenge her father's death.

After the death of her father, Oiwa, grief-stricken and vulnerable, chose to remain with Iemon. In due course, she became pregnant and gave birth to a son. However, the family's financial struggles deepened, and Oiwa's health took a severe turn post-childbirth. As she grew weaker, Iemon's frustration and resentment toward her intensified.

During this turbulent period, Iemon crossed paths with Oume, the youthful and attractive granddaughter of Ito Kihei, a wealthy and influential doctor. Oume, captivated by Iemon despite his marital status, fell deeply in love with him. Her grandfather, cherishing Oume dearly, resolved to ensure her happiness at any cost. Together, they schemed to remove Oiwa from Iemon's life, allowing Oume to take her place.

Jealous of Oiwa's beauty and her position as Iemon's wife, Oume and her grandfather conspired to ruin her. Ito Kihei, feigning benevolence, provided Oiwa with an ointment he claimed would restore her health. In truth, it was a poison intended to disfigure her. As days passed, Oiwa's condition deteriorated. Her once beautiful face became grotesquely scarred, and her hair fell out in clumps. Witnessing Oiwa's transformation, Iemon's feelings turned from resentment to outright hatred.

"Iemon, my love, is the ointment working?" Oiwa asked, hoping that her condition was improving.

Iemon, unable to hide his revulsion, replied coldly, "Yes, Oiwa, keep using it."

Seeing his opportunity, Ito Kihei suggested that Iemon divorce Oiwa and marry Oume instead. "Marry my granddaughter, and you will inherit our family's wealth," he promised.

Entranced by Oume's beauty and repulsed by Oiwa's appearance, Iemon agreed. After all, Oume was younger than his wife, and her grandfather's wealth was indeed enticing. He began selling Oiwa's belongings, including her kimono and their son's clothes, to gather funds for his new marriage. However, another problem lingered: he needed a legitimate reason to divorce Oiwa. Desperate, Iemon enlisted his friend Takuetsu to assault Oiwa so he could accuse her of infidelity.

On the planned night, while Iemon was away, Takuetsu entered their home and approached Oiwa. But the sight of Oiwa's disfigured face surprised him, and he had a change of heart— Takuetsu could not carry on with the plan. And so, he chose to tell poor Oiwa the truth.

"Apologies will never be enough, Oiwa. But at the very least, let me tell you the truth," Takuetsu confessed, his voice trembling. "Iemon orchestrated this. He wanted me to violate you so he could claim you were unfaithful."

Devastated, Oiwa looked at herself in the mirror for the first time since using the ointment. She saw a monstrous reflection staring back at her. In a desperate attempt to cover her scars, she brushed her hair over her face, only for it to fall out in bloody clumps. Overwhelmed by betrayal and her horrific appearance, Oiwa grabbed Takuetsu's sword to take her own life. Takuetsu tried to stop her but failed. In just moments, Oiwa dropped to the floor, surrounded by a pool of blood.

Iemon seeing Oiwa's ghostly face on lanterns.[4]

As Oiwa lay dying, she cursed Iemon with her final breaths. Iemon's servant, Kohei, later discovered her body and reported the news. Instead of grief, Iemon felt relief and joy. Kohei, suspecting foul play, confronted Iemon but was killed and disposed of alongside Oiwa. Iemon fabricated a story that Kohei and Oiwa were lovers, freeing himself to marry Oume.

From there on, Oiwa's curse swiftly took effect. On the first night after marrying Oume, Iemon was plagued by a feeling of uneasiness. He had trouble sleeping, so he rolled on his side to look at his new wife. Much to his horror, it was not Oume by his side, but his disfigured late wife. In a panic, he slashed out with his sword, only to realize he had killed Oume and the sight of Oiwa was nothing more than an illusion. Terrified, he sought help from Ito Kihei but was confronted by Kohei's ghost. In his frenzy, Iemon swung his sword again. Once the illusion ended, he discovered that he had also killed Ito Kihei.

Haunted by Oiwa's vengeful spirit, Iemon fled into the night. She appeared everywhere—in his dreams, shadows, and even the lanterns lighting his way. Driven mad by her relentless pursuit, Iemon sought refuge in the mountains, but even there, Oiwa's ghost found him. Unable to distinguish reality from nightmare, Iemon descended into madness.

The Peony Lantern Ghost Story

The third story of the Nihon san dai kaidan begins on the night of the Obon festival when the air is thick with the scent of incense and the soft glow of lanterns. This annual event, held to honor and welcome the spirits of ancestors back to Earth for a few days, is a deeply significant time in Japanese culture. Families prepare by cleaning their homes, offering food, and lighting lanterns to guide their loved ones' spirits. It is a time of reverence and reunion, where the boundary between the living and the dead blurs.

However, amidst the joyous reunions of one Obon festival, one man chose not to participate. Ogiwara Shinnojo, recently bereaved of his wife, remained in his house, enveloped in grief. As the festival carried on outside, Ogiwara sat alone, his heart heavy with sorrow.

In the distance, he noticed a faint light. As it drew nearer, he could see it was coming from a lantern. The lantern, adorned with painted peony flowers, was carried by a woman who appeared to be a servant. Beside her walked another woman whose beauty was so striking it left Ogiwara almost speechless. He rose to greet them, his curiosity piqued by their mysterious presence.

The beautiful woman introduced herself as Otsuyu, and the woman carrying the lantern was her servant. They explained that they had just come from a nearby temple. Enchanted by Otsuyu's beauty and the sense of calm she brought, Ogiwara invited them into his home. They talked, laughed, and enjoyed each other's company late into the night. When Otsuyu left before dawn, Ogiwara felt a pang of sadness at her departure.

To his surprise, Otsuyu returned the following night. Once again, they spent the night together, sharing stories, laughter, and eventually the bed. This routine continued for several nights, and Ogiwara found himself falling deeply in love. His days became a mere prelude to the nights he spent with Otsuyu. He barely left his home, consumed by anticipation for her next visit.

However, Ogiwara's peculiar behavior did not go unnoticed. Concerned, a neighbor decided to check on him one evening. Hearing eerie laughter from within, the neighbor peeked inside and was horrified by what he saw. Ogiwara was not with a

Otsuyu and her servant.[42]

beautiful woman but with a decomposing corpse, its skeletal form barely covered with decaying flesh.

The next day, the neighbor confronted Ogiwara, explaining the ghastly sight he had witnessed. Shocked and disbelieving, Ogiwara listened as the neighbor urged him to stop meeting Otsuyu. "She will drain your life away," the neighbor warned. "You must break free from her spell."

Determined to uncover the truth, Ogiwara recalled that Otsuyu had mentioned coming from a nearby temple. He ventured to the temple and, sure enough, found a peony lantern lying atop a grave. His heart sank as he realized that Otsuyu had died long ago, before they had met. Ogiwara recounted his experience to a Buddhist priest, who provided him with a spirit-repelling charm to place outside his home. That night, Otsuyu did not return.

Despite the charm's effectiveness, Ogiwara's longing for Otsuyu only grew. Consumed by sadness and desperation, he turned to alcohol for solace. One fateful night, in a drunken haze, Ogiwara stumbled to the temple and made his way to Otsuyu's grave. There, she appeared before him, as beautiful as ever. Otsuyu invited him to stay with her, and, overwhelmed by love and longing, Ogiwara agreed.

Ogiwara was never seen again. When the priest decided to open Otsuyu's grave, he discovered two bodies lying together: Ogiwara, embracing the decomposed remains of Otsuyu.

Legends say that on dark, cloudy nights, people would sometimes see Otsuyu, her servant, and Ogiwara Shinnojo walking together. Those who saw them would fall ill, prompting rituals to release the three spirits from the earthly realm forever.

The Peony Lantern stands apart from the other two ghost stories of the Nihon san dai kaidan in its emotional core. While the stories of Okiku and Oiwa are driven by fierce vengeance, Otsuyu's lingering spirit is fueled by profound loneliness.

These ghost tales hold deep cultural significance, reflecting societal norms, fears, and the collective psyche regarding death, loyalty, love, and retribution. They provide thrilling and chilling narratives that offer insights into traditional Japanese concepts of life and the afterlife, illustrating how the past continuously informs the present. Through these stories, we explore the consequences of betrayal, the power of love, and the inevitability of death.

Ghost stories are integral to festivals like Obon, where spirits are honored and remembered. These stories have also permeated literature, highlighting their enduring popularity and influence on Japanese art and entertainment.

Ghost Tales in Japanese Theaters

Ghost stories find a prominent place in theater, especially in Noh and Kabuki, where the haunting tales come to life on stage, captivating audiences with their eerie beauty. Kabuki is a classical Japanese dance-drama known for its highly stylized performances, vibrant costumes, and elaborate makeup. Originating in the early seventeenth century, Kabuki was initially performed by female dancers, but it evolved to become an all-male art form. Kabuki plays often include dramatic plots, historical events, and supernatural elements.

The story of Oiwa from *Tōkaidō Yotsuya Kaidan* is one of the most famous ghost stories performed in Kabuki, where the elaborate staging and intense acting bring the tragic and vengeful spirit to life, captivating audiences with its horror and emotional depth. The story of Oiwa is performed with dramatic flair, using special effects to create ghostly apparitions and chilling scenes. The elaborate sets, lighting, and makeup enhance the eerie atmosphere, making the audience feel the horror of Oiwa's vengeance.

Kabuki actors dressed as samurai.[43]

Noh, on the other hand, is a more refined and minimalist form of theater that dates to the fourteenth century. It combines music, dance, and acting to create a highly stylized performance. Noh plays often explore themes of the supernatural, with ghosts and spirits frequently taking center stage. The actors wear intricate masks and costumes, and the performances are accompanied by traditional music. The story of Okiku from *Banchō Sarayashiki* is a classic example of a ghost tale in Noh, where the haunting presence of Okiku, wronged in life, is portrayed with subtlety and grace, evoking a sense of melancholy and spiritual unrest. The use of masks and minimalist stage design helps to convey the tragic beauty of Okiku's spirit, creating a hauntingly poignant performance.

Both Kabuki and Noh have adapted the story of the Peony Lantern, highlighting the tragic love story between Ogiwara and the ghostly Otsuyu. In Kabuki, the costumes and acting emphasize the romantic and supernatural elements, while in Noh, the story is told with a more subdued and introspective approach.

The integration of these tales into festivals, literature, and theatrical performances like Noh and Kabuki illustrates their enduring popularity and influence on Japanese culture and art. Through these stories, audiences are reminded of the thin veil between life and death and the timeless emotions that bind humanity across generations.

Chapter 9 – Wisdom of the Elders

An old man and his wife lived in a small village. Their life was one of simplicity and hardship, woven together by their daily labor. As the end of the year approached, the world around them was transformed by a blanket of thick snow. The air grew bitterly cold.

The old couple earned their meager living by weaving straw hats. Every day, they worked tirelessly, their hands moving deftly as they crafted the hats with care and skill. By the end of this particular day, they had managed to weave five straw hats, hoping to sell them in the town the next day. As the old man put down the last hat, he sighed deeply. "Wife," he lamented, "the new year is almost

An example of a Japanese straw hat.“

upon us, and yet we have no rice cakes to celebrate. It has been years since we've had any to mark the occasion."

In Japan, the new year, or Oshōgatsu, is a time of great importance. It is a season for family, for renewing hope and joy, and for starting afresh. Rice cakes, or mochi, symbolize prosperity and good fortune.

The absence of these simple treats made the couple's poverty all the starker. The old woman, however, looked at her husband with gentle optimism. "Tomorrow, you will go to town and sell these straw hats," she said. "With the earnings, we shall buy rice cakes and welcome the new year properly."

Comforted by her words, the old man nodded, and they went to sleep, clinging to the fragile hope of a better tomorrow.

The next morning, the old man set off for the town, carrying the five straw hats. He trudged through the thick snow, braving the freezing air with each step. As he arrived in town, he called out to passersby, trying to sell the hats. Unfortunately, no one was interested.

With a heavy heart, the old man began his long journey back home, his hopes dashed. The snow seemed thicker and the cold more biting. As he walked along the foot of the mountain, he came across a row of six Jizo statues. The old man, known for his compassionate heart, stopped and looked at the statues.

A row of Jizo statues.[45]

"Ah, you poor things," he murmured. "Though you are statues, surely you must feel the cold as we do." He decided to use the straw hats to cover the heads of the Jizo statues. One by one, he placed the hats upon them until he came to the last statue. Realizing he only had five hats, he removed his own hat and placed it on the final statue. Smiling at his deed, he continued his journey home.

When he arrived, his wife was waiting for him, worry etched on her face. "Husband, where is your hat? You must be freezing!" she exclaimed.

The old man recounted his encounter with the Jizo statues and how he had given away their straw hats, along with his own. His wife listened, pride welling up in her heart. "Your compassion is admirable," she said. "We may not have rice cakes, but we have each other's company, and that is what truly matters."

They spent the new year's eve in the simplest of ways, without rice cakes, but with the warmth of their companionship. As they drifted off to sleep, they were content.

In the middle of the night, they were awakened by distant voices singing about the old man's kind act. The singing grew louder, and suddenly, there was a thud outside their door. The couple jumped out of bed and hurried to see what had happened. To their astonishment, they found the freshest rice cakes, neatly arranged on a straw mat, placed right in front of their door.

"Who could have done this?" the old man wondered aloud. He noticed tracks in the snow and decided to follow them. He traced the tracks back to the six Jizo statues, still wearing the hats he had given them. To his amazement, the statues were walking across the snow.

Delighted, he rushed back to his wife. "It was the Jizo statues! They have rewarded us for our kindness," he exclaimed.

His wife smiled, her eyes shining with happiness. "Thanks to your compassion, we can enjoy the rice cakes and have a wonderful new year celebration after all."

And so, the old couple enjoyed a joyous new year, their hearts warmed by the kindness and gratitude they had experienced.

In Japanese belief, Jizo statues are protectors of children, travelers, and the souls of the deceased. They are revered for their role as compassionate guardians. This tale of the grateful statues teaches us that acts of kindness, no matter how small, are never forgotten and often return to us in ways we least expect.

The wisdom of elders is a theme that runs deep in Japanese folktales. Rooted in centuries-old traditions, these moral tales have been passed down from generation to generation, serving not only as entertainment but as tools for teaching and reinforcing societal values. They highlight virtues like compassion, honesty, and humility, weaving them into the fabric of daily life. Through simple yet profound stories, elders impart wisdom, guiding the young and reminding the old of the principles that bind their community together.

There is also a tale that teaches the dangers of greed. This story, known as "The Tongue-Cut Sparrow," also took place in a quiet countryside village, where yet another couple lived. While the husband was kind-hearted and soft-spoken, his wife was a tempestuous woman, bad-tempered and with a tongue like a sword. Her words could pierce through anyone's spirit, leaving them bruised and battered.

The husband longed for a child, but his ill-tempered wife wished for none. Whenever he tried to persuade her, she would scold and shout at him until he relented. To soothe his yearning for a child, the man kept a sparrow as a pet. He cared for the bird with all his heart, feeding it by hand and spending time with it. His wife, seeing the affection her husband lavished on the sparrow, despised the bird terribly.

The wife was especially foul tempered on wash days. Her youth had long faded, and now her back and knees protested the arduous task of kneeling to wash clothes. One day, she mixed some starch and placed it in a bowl to cool, preparing to wash the clothes. Suddenly, the sparrow came and pecked at the starch. In a fit of rage, the wife grabbed the poor bird and cut off its tongue, then flung it into the air, shouting, "Never come back!"

When her husband returned, he searched the entire house for his beloved pet. With a heavy heart, he asked his wife what had happened. She recounted every detail, and the man's sadness deepened. He searched for the sparrow day and night, but when he couldn't find it, he gave up hope. One day, as he wandered the mountains, he came across his beloved sparrow. The bird recognized him, and after exchanging bows and greetings, the man expressed how much he had missed his pet. The sparrow invited him to its new home, and the man, delighted, agreed.

The sparrow had built a new life for itself, with a wife and two daughters. It introduced its family to the old man, who was overjoyed for his pet. They spent days together, talking, playing Go—a game of strategy played with black and white stones on a wooden board—and laughing. It was a wonderful time for both.

After several days, the man decided it was time to return home. The sparrow, though sad to see him go, was grateful for the visit. As a token of gratitude, the sparrow offered the man a parting gift. It placed two baskets before him—one heavier than the other—and asked him to choose. Aware of his age and limited strength, the man chose the lighter basket, saying it would be easier to carry down the mountain path. And so they parted, the man carrying the lighter basket home.

When he arrived, his wife greeted him with a barrage of angry words. She was furious that he had been gone for days. The man begged her to stop scolding, and she reluctantly obliged. He then recounted his visit to the sparrow's home and the kindness shown to him. When he opened the basket, they found it filled with gold, coral, precious gems, and other valuables. His wife's eyes gleamed with greed. She declared that she, too, would visit the sparrow to receive a gift.

The wife's visit was far from pleasant. The sparrow was not delighted to see her, but out of politeness, it invited her into its home. Unlike her husband, she did not receive the same hospitality. When she expressed her wish to leave, the sparrow did not offer any gift. Nevertheless, she insisted. The sparrow eventually presented her with two baskets—one heavier than the other. Greedily, she chose the heavier basket and began her journey home. Impatient, she opened the basket to see her treasures.

Instead of gold and gems, a swarm of goblins, a horned oni, and a serpent sprang from the basket. The serpent coiled around her, cracking her bones until she met her end.

The husband, after burying his wife, adopted a son. With the wealth he now possessed, the father and son lived happily ever after.

While the tale of the grateful Jizo statues tells the lesson of kindness, this tale about the tongue-cut sparrow teaches the peril of greed. In seeking more than one's share, one may find oneself entangled in misfortune and suffering.

Another lesson usually found in these age-old folktales is the peril of unbridled desire. Desires can drive people to reach for more than they need, often leading them away from true happiness and satisfaction. The constant yearning for something greater can blind one to the simple joys of their current life.

A Warning about Desire

Once upon a time, there lived a humble stonecutter. Every day, he would chisel away at large stones by the mountainside, shaping them into slabs for gravestones and houses. For the longest time, he was happy and content, asking for nothing more than what he had.

Unbeknownst to the stonecutter, the mountain where he worked was the dwelling of a spirit, who would occasionally appear before human eyes. The stonecutter had heard stories of this spirit, but he never believed them. That was about to change.

One day, as the stonecutter carried his stones to a house belonging to a rich man, he was overwhelmed by desire. He stared at the house, wondering, "How would it feel to live such an easy life?" From that day on, he lost interest in his work, thinking life would be easier if he did not have to do heavy labor yet still enjoyed luxury. "I wish I were a rich man," he muttered, believing he would be much happier.

The mountain spirit heard his wish and, with a distant voice, granted it. "Your wish is granted," the spirit intoned.

The stonecutter, finding no one around, shrugged it off and went home, only to find his house transformed into a grand mansion. Ecstatic, he indulged in his new life, forgetting his old ways.

Later, summer came, and with it, new desires. He saw a prince arriving in town, shaded by servants holding umbrellas. "How wonderful it would be to be a prince," he thought, "shielded from this scorching heat." So, he wished to be a prince, and the mountain spirit granted this wish as well.

Living as a prince, the stonecutter felt powerful, but his heart still yearned for more. Looking up, he saw the sun, which could dry rivers and scorch the earth. "The sun is mightier," he thought. "I wish to be the sun."

Again, the spirit granted his wish. As the sun, he scorched the land and tormented everyone until a cloud blocked his rays. Frustrated, he realized even the sun was not all-powerful. "I wish to be the cloud," he declared.

As a cloud, he blocked the sun and poured rain, causing floods that destroyed villages and palaces alike. Yet, a great rock by the mountainside remained unscathed. "That rock is mightier than I," he mused. "I wish to be the rock."

Transformed into the great rock, he felt invincible. But one day, another stonecutter approached. With his tools, the stonecutter chipped away at him, causing a huge slab to fall. Powerless, the rock could only watch. "How can this tiny man be more powerful than a rock?" he cried. "I wish to be my old self again!"

The mountain spirit, with a touch of amusement, granted this final wish.

Back in his humble form, the stonecutter realized the folly of his desires. "I do not need to wish to be something greater," he thought. "I must be satisfied and grateful for what I have."

From that day forward, he never wished for things he did not have. Instead, he cherished what he already possessed, understanding that true happiness comes from contentment and gratitude.

The Obasute: The Mythical Practice of Elderly Abandonment

In medieval Japan, there was a practice known as obasute (or ubasute), in which elderly people were taken to the mountains and abandoned. This cruel tradition was rooted in the belief that the elderly, unable to perform heavy labor, consumed precious resources without contributing significantly to the community.

One such tale of obasute involves a young farmer and his aged mother. They lived under the rule of a particularly heartless lord, who decreed that anyone who reached the age of seventy must be taken to the mountains and left to die. The elderly were seen as burdens, their wisdom undervalued compared to their daily consumption of rice.

When the farmer's mother turned seventy, she knew the time had come. "My dearest son," she said gently, "you must take me to the mountains. It is the lord's decree."

The young farmer's heart ached at the thought. "Mother, I cannot do such a thing. You have cared for me all my life."

"You must," she insisted, "for the lord's wrath will be severe if we disobey."

With great reluctance and a heavy heart, the young farmer agreed. He carried his mother on his back, ascending the steep, rocky path. Along the way, she quietly snapped twigs from the trees and dropped them behind them.

"Mother, why do you break the twigs?" he asked.

"So that you may find your way back home," she replied. Her words brought tears to his eyes. Moved by her selflessness even in the face of death, the young farmer could not bear to leave her. He turned back and brought his mother home, hiding her in a secret room he dug beneath their house.

A depiction of a young man carrying his mother up Obasute Mountain.[46]

The village soon faced a new threat. An ambitious lord sought to conquer their land, and he issued a challenge to the cruel village lord: produce a rope made of ash, and the village would be spared. If they failed, the village would fall.

Desperate to save his people and preserve his power, the cruel lord gathered the villagers and asked if anyone knew how to create such a rope. None could provide an answer. The young farmer, anxious to help, consulted his hidden mother.

The old woman thought for a moment and then said, "Wet some straw with salty water and weave it into a rope. Let it dry, then burn it carefully. The ash will hold the shape of the rope."

Following her instructions, the young farmer created the ash rope and presented it to the cruel lord. Astonished, the lord asked, "How did you, a mere farmer, come up with such wisdom?"

The young man confessed, "It was not my wisdom, but my mother's. She is still alive, hidden in my home."

Realizing the depth of his error, the cruel lord saw the invaluable wisdom of the elderly. He revoked the decree, declaring, "Now that our village is safe again, let it be known that no elder shall be abandoned again. Their knowledge and experience are treasures that we must honor and protect."

Chapter 10 – Key Symbols of Japanese Folklore

Japanese folklore is full of symbols and motifs that reveal deeper truths about life, nature, and humanity. Usually, these symbols are intricately woven into stories, providing lessons and guidance to those who pay attention.

For example, most people cannot help but think of cherry blossoms when they hear the word Japan. This is fair, as cherry blossoms are more than just flowers in the eyes of the Japanese. These sakura flowers bloom in the spring, bringing joy to all who see them. But their beauty is fleeting, reminding us that life itself is short and precious. Every year, families and friends gather under the blooming trees, celebrating the tradition of hanami, or flower viewing. They laugh, share stories, and enjoy the moment, knowing that the blossoms will soon fall. Through these tales, the cherry blossoms teach us to cherish each day and appreciate the beauty around us.

This deep connection to the sakura is reflected in countless stories and poems in which the blossoms are celebrated for their beauty and the profound lessons they teach about the cycle of life.

Cherry blossoms at Mount Yoshino.⁴⁷

One such story tells of a samurai who would sit beneath the cherry trees, contemplating the impermanence of life. The falling petals reminded him of the fragility of existence and the importance of living honorably and fully. This tale, like many others, illustrates how the cherry blossom is a powerful symbol of beauty and ephemerality, teaching the value of mindfulness and presence.

Meanwhile, in the rivers and streams, koi fish swim with all their might against the strong currents. The koi fish, or carp, is a symbol of luck, perseverance, and strength in Japanese culture. During festivals, people celebrate the koi's journey as it struggles upstream, symbolizing the ability to overcome life's challenges. On the annual Children's Day festival, families fly koi-shaped windsocks, called koinobori, to celebrate the hope that their children will grow up to be as strong and determined as the koi. There are stories of koi transforming into powerful dragons, showing that determination and hard work can lead to great transformation and success. These tales encourage us to be resilient no matter how difficult our path may be.

The folding fan, with its graceful curves and intricate designs, is another symbol with meaning. Known as sensu, or ogi, the folding fan symbolizes the unfolding of future possibilities and the elegance of life's journey. Fans are often given as gifts to convey good wishes and the hope for a bright future. The act of opening a fan is a metaphor for revealing hidden potential and embracing new opportunities.

The fan's delicate design and graceful movements in traditional Japanese dance and ceremonies tell stories of beauty, status, and good fortune. Each flick of the fan can reveal a new scene or emotion, making it a versatile tool for storytelling and expression.

A Japanese folding fan from the Heian period.[48]

In many folktales, a fan plays a crucial role. One popular story tells of a young maiden who, with the help of a magical fan, was able to reveal hidden treasures and secrets. This tale, like many others, shows the power of the fan as a symbol of guidance.

Mythical creatures also play a significant role in Japanese folklore. Dragons, revered for their power and strength, are seen as protectors and guardians of nature. The dragon's ability to control the weather and the seas highlights their role as powerful yet compassionate beings. In festivals, dragon dances celebrate their might and bring good fortune to communities. Stories of dragons emphasize their protective nature, showing us that true strength lies in safeguarding and nurturing those around us.

Nature itself is imbued with symbolism in Japanese folklore. Water, for instance, is a symbol of purity and change. It purifies and sustains life, and its flow represents the constant movement and transformation of existence. Rivers, lakes, and the sea are often depicted as homes to spirits like the kappa, who embody the dual nature of water—both life-giving and potentially dangerous. These stories teach us to respect and honor the natural world, understanding its vital role in our lives. The ever-changing nature of water reminds us that life is fluid and we must adapt to its flow.

Mountains hold a sacred place in Japanese culture. These towering peaks are worshiped and revered, as they are seen as abodes of gods and spirits. Pilgrimages to sacred mountains are common. Folktales often feature mountain deities who test the resolve of characters, guiding them toward personal growth and enlightenment.

Forests, with their dense foliage and hidden depths, symbolize mystery and life. They are home to spirits like the kodama, which inhabit trees and watch over the woods. Forests in folklore are places of both danger and refuge.

All of these symbols offer moral lessons, guiding characters to make ethical choices and embrace virtues like courage, compassion, and humility. They serve as cautionary elements, highlighting the perils of greed, pride, and disrespect for nature.

In Japanese folklore, symbols also play an important role in the concept of "mono no aware," the awareness of the impermanence of things. This concept is deeply ingrained in Japanese culture and is reflected in the appreciation of fleeting moments of beauty, such as the blooming of cherry blossoms or the passing of seasons. The symbols in these tales often evoke a sense of wistfulness and appreciation for the transient nature of life. They teach us to find beauty in impermanence and to live with a mindful awareness of the present.

In the end, these symbols and stories serve as bridges between the tangible and spiritual worlds. They connect us to the natural order and offer insights into human behavior. They remind us that we are part of a larger world, held together by shared experiences, values, and dreams. As we journey through life, these symbols guide us, teaching us to live with respect, gratitude, and awareness.

Conclusion

As our journey through Japanese folktales and legends draws to a close, it becomes clear that these stories are far more than echoes from an ancient past. In every tale, themes that resonate deeply with the human spirit emerge, touching upon the eternal values that bind humanity together.

These folktales reveal the profound respect held for nature in Japanese culture. Through tales of kami, spirits inhabiting everything from the mightiest mountains to the smallest streams, the natural world is shown to be sacred and alive. Stories of the kappa and the sacred camphor tree at Kayashima Station remind us that every element of nature is imbued with life and deserves respect.

Loyalty and honor shine through many of these tales, especially in the legends of samurai like Miyamoto Musashi and the forty-seven ronin. These stories of valor and sacrifice demonstrate that true strength lies not in might but in unwavering dedication to principles. The story of the forty-seven ronin, who avenged the death of their master at great personal cost, speaks to the timeless values of loyalty and courage.

The wisdom embedded in these folktales transcends time, offering insights into the human condition. Themes of love, sacrifice, courage, and cunning are explored. The tale of Urashima Taro, for instance, reflects on the fleeting nature of time and the consequences of actions, urging thoughtful choices and cherishing every moment. These stories encourage looking beyond the surface to seek the deeper truths that guide us toward a more meaningful existence.

In a fast-paced modern world, the lessons from these ancient stories emphasize slowing down and reflecting on life. These tales are guides that help us navigate the challenges of contemporary life, whether through respecting nature, upholding honor, or acting with kindness and empathy.

These stories also bridge the gap between cultures, offering a glimpse into Japan's rich heritage and the values that have shaped its society. The universal themes of love, honor, and the supernatural transcend cultural boundaries, allowing connections with others on a profound level. Through these tales, a broader perspective on traditions and values is gained, enriching our understanding of the world.

Japanese folktales also inspire creativity, influencing countless works of art, literature, and cinema. The imagery and profound themes found in these stories continue to captivate artists and writers, providing a wellspring of ideas that can be reimagined in new and innovative ways.

As the final pages of this book close, it becomes evident that Japanese folktales are timeless treasures, offering lessons that are as valuable today as they were in the past. They remind all to live in harmony with nature, to uphold honor and loyalty, and to seek wisdom in daily life. Let these stories inspire stewardship of the earth, actions of integrity, and cherishing the wisdom passed down through generations. The legacy of these folktales lives on, guiding with timeless truths and enriching lives in ways that are both profound and enduring. These stories will continue to captivate and inspire, showcasing the power of storytelling to shape our understanding of the world and humanity's place within it.

If you enjoyed this book, a review on Amazon would be greatly appreciated because it would mean a lot to hear from you.

To leave a review:

1. Open your camera app.
2. Point your mobile device at the QR code.
3. The review page will appear in your web browser.

Thanks for your support!

Here's another book by Enthralling History that you might like

Free limited time bonus

Stop for a moment. We have a free bonus set up for you. The problem is this: we forget 90% of everything that we read after 7 days. Crazy fact, right? Here's the solution: we've created a printable, 1-page pdf summary for this book that you're reading now. All you have to do to get your free pdf summary is to go to the following website: https://livetolearn.lpages.co/enthrallinghistory/

Or, Scan the QR code!

Once you do, it will be intuitive. Enjoy, and thank you!

Bibliography

"About Inari-Okami," *Spirit Fox* (blog), May 31, 2022.
https://spiritfoxtarot.wordpress.com/my-patron-inari/.

Barsotyi, Marty. "People From Japanese Lore: Yamato Takeru." *Wasshoi*,
November 9, 2021. https://www.wasshoimagazine.org/blog/discovering-
japan/yamato-takeru.

Cartwright, Mark, and Taku. "Izanami and Izanagi." *World History
Encyclopedia*, July 2, 2024.
https://www.worldhistory.org/Izanami_and_Izanagi/.

Cavendish, Richard. "The Forty-Seven Ronin Incident." *History Today*,
December 12, 2002. https://www.historytoday.com/archive/months-past/forty-
seven-ronin-incident.

Copeland, Rebecca. "Yamamba: The Japanese Mountain Witch." *Medium*,
February 12, 2022. https://medium.com/japonica-publication/yamamba-the-
japanese-mountain-witch-b1e13262300b.

De Lange, William. "Arima Kihei." *Miyamoto Musashi* (blog), accessed June
18, 2024. http://www.miyamotomusashi.eu/duels/arima-kihei.html.

"Fourth Century: The Legend of Prince Yamatotakeru: The Path He Took
and Yamato's Expansion," *Heritage of Japan* (blog), February 4, 2009.
https://heritageofjapan.wordpress.com/following-the-trail-of-tumuli/4th-century-
the-legend-of-prince-yamatotakeru-the-path-he-took-and-yamatos-expansion/.

Frydman, Joshua. *The Japanese Myths: A Guide to Gods, Heroes and Spirits*.
National Geographic Books, 2022.

Griffis, William Elliot. "The Tongue-Cut Sparrow: A Fairy Tale From Japan,"
Professor D.L. Ashliman (University of Pittsburgh), last modified April 5,
2015. https://sites.pitt.edu/~dash/sparrow.html.

Japonais, Katana. "Samurai and Their Relationship With the Katana: History and Anecdotes." *Katana Sword* (blog), April 7, 2023. https://katana-sword.com/blogs/katana-blog/samurai-and-their-relationship-with-the-katana-history-and-anecdotes.

Kimball, Donny. "The Myth Shuten Doji | Kyoto's Mt. Oe & the 'Drunken Demon.'" *A Different Side of Japan* (blog), December 2, 2023. https://donnykimball.com/shuten-doji-mt-oe-8334ec2dd479.

Kincaid, Chris. "The Stonecutter." *Japan Powered* (blog), May 23, 2016. https://www.japanpowered.com/folklore-and-urban-legends/stonecutter.

Kondo, Daniel. "Princess Kaguya | a Tale for the Ages." Japan House (Los Angeles), September 9, 2021. https://www.japanhousela.com/articles/princess-kaguya-a-tale-for-the-ages/.

Linfamy. "Yokai Explained: Tofu Boy (Don't Eat What He Gives You)." YouTube video, 4:33, November 27, 2021. https://www.youtube.com/watch?v=-s_vQ_W73qo.

Lye, Sian. "Volcanoes: What Are They?" Japan National Tourism Association, accessed June 11, 2024. https://www.japan.travel/national-parks/plan-your-visit/guides-and-stories/volcanoes-what-are-they/#:~:text=Japan's%20volcanoes%20are%20largely%20formed,by%2Dproduct%20of%20volcanic%20activity.

Masanobu, Kagawa. "'Tengu': The Birdlike Demons That Became Almost Divine." Nippon Communications Foundation, December 2, 2022. https://www.nippon.com/en/japan-topics/b02507/.

Matsui, Alana. "Scary Stories: 7 Japanese Tales That Will Chill You to the Bone." *Savvy Tokyo*, February 6, 2024. https://savvytokyo.com/scary-stories-7-japanese-tales-that-will-chill-you-to-the-bone/.

"Mt. Ibuki." Omi Tourism Board, February 21, 2020. https://visit-omi.com/poi/article/mt-ibuki.

Meyer, Matthew. "Hōsōgami." Yokai.com GK, accessed June 24, 2024. https://yokai.com/housougami/.

Meyer, Matthew. "Oiwa." Yokai.com GK, accessed June 25, 2024. https://yokai.com/oiwa/.

Meyer, Matthew. "Okiku." Yokai.com GK, accessed June 25, 2024. https://yokai.com/okiku/.

Meyer, Matthew. "Toyotama Hime." Yokai.com GK, accessed June 21, 2024. https://yokai.com/toyotamahime/.

Meyer, Matthew. "Yamabiko." Yokai.com GK, accessed June 27, 2024. https://yokai.com/yamabiko/.

Naoki, Matsumoto. "Amaterasu: The Japanese Sun Goddess." Nippon.com, July 1, 2023. https://www.nippon.com/en/japan-topics/g00748/amaterasu-the-japanese-sun-goddess.html.

Rinpoche, H.E. Tsem. "Kappa – the Japanese Water Demon | 河童 ー 日本水怪," Tsem Rinpoche, February 21, 2024. https://www.tsemrinpoche.com/tsem-tulku-rinpoche/one-minute-story/kappa-the-japanese-water-demon.

Strusiewicz, Cezary Jan. "How Women Disappeared From Kabuki Theater | Tokyo Weekender." *Tokyo Weekender*, January 10, 2022. https://www.tokyoweekender.com/art_and_culture/japanese-culture/no-women-kabuki-theater-japan/.

"The Legendary Duel Between Sasaki Kojiro and Miyamoto Musashi." *The Archaeologist: Civilizations of the World* (blog), November 15, 2022. https://www.thearchaeologist.org/blog/the-legendary-duel-between-sasaki-kojiro-and-miyamoto-musashi.

"The History of Miyamoto Musashi." Niten Institute, accessed June 15, 2024. https://m.niten.org/english/instituto/miyamoto_musashi/musashi-biografia.

"The Myths of Japan: Into the Underworld." Miyazaki Prefecture Tourism Association, accessed June 13, 2024. https://visitmiyazaki.com/mythology/into-the-underworld/.

"The Story of Kiyohime." Tenabe International English Guide Association (TIEGA), accessed June 21, 2024. https://tekutekutb.kiiminpo.jp/cnts2/lw/?db=tiega&mode=tiega&id=241020&name=The+Story+of+Kiyohime.

"Tsuru No Ongaeshi – Japanese Folktale." *Kyuhoshi* (blog), updated April 9, 2024. https://www.kyuhoshi.com/tsuru-no-ongaeshi/.

Uchida, Yoskiko. "The Wise Old Woman." | *Kirkus Reviews*," October 1, 1994. https://www.kirkusreviews.com/book-reviews/yoshiko-uchida/the-wise-old-woman/.

Wright, Gregory. "Inari." Mythopedia, December 6, 2022. https://mythopedia.com/topics/inari.

Image Sources

[1] *Boccaccio1, CC BY 2.0 <https://creativecommons.org/licenses/by/2.0>, via Wikimedia Commons: https://commons.wikimedia.org/wiki/File:Yotei_Volcano_on_Hokkaido_in_Japan_20101025.jpg*

[2] *https://commons.wikimedia.org/wiki/File:Izanagi_and_Izanami_giving_birth_to_Japan_c1870_after_Kawanabe_Kyosai.jpg*

[3] *https://commons.wikimedia.org/wiki/File:Japan_Map_CIA_2021.png*

[4] *ChiefHira, CC BY-SA 3.0 <https://creativecommons.org/licenses/by-sa/3.0>, via Wikimedia Commons: https://commons.wikimedia.org/wiki/File:Yomotsu_Hirasaka.JPG*

[5] *Brigham Young University, CC BY-SA 4.0 <https://creativecommons.org/licenses/by-sa/4.0>, via Wikimedia Commons: https://commons.wikimedia.org/wiki/File:30.Yukionna.jpg*

[6] *A.Davey from Portland, Oregon, EE UU, CC BY 2.0 <https://creativecommons.org/licenses/by/2.0>, via Wikimedia Commons: https://commons.wikimedia.org/wiki/File:Two_Women_rinse_the_hands_(act_of_misogi_using_temizu)_(1915-01_by_Elstner_Hilton).jpg*

[7] *I, KENPEI, CC BY-SA 3.0 <http://creativecommons.org/licenses/by-sa/3.0>, via Wikimedia Commons: https://commons.wikimedia.org/wiki/File:Hushimi-inari-taisha_omotesando.jpg*

[8] *DVMG, CC BY 3.0 <https://creativecommons.org/licenses/by/3.0>, via Wikimedia Commons: https://commons.wikimedia.org/wiki/File:Keihan_Kayashima_Station_platform_-_panoramio_(11).jpg*

[9] *en.Wikipedia: Werewolf, CC BY-SA 3.0 <http://creativecommons.org/licenses/by-sa/3.0>, via Wikimedia Commons: https://commons.wikimedia.org/wiki/File:Inuyama_inari_1.jpg*

[10] *Marco Almbauer, CC BY-SA 4.0 <https://creativecommons.org/licenses/by-sa/4.0>, via Wikimedia Commons: https://commons.wikimedia.org/wiki/File:Torii,_Fushimi_Inari-Taisha.jpg*

[11] https://commons.wikimedia.org/wiki/File:Wind_God_and_Thunder_God_Screens_by_Tawaraya_Sotatsu_hi-res.png

[12] https://commons.wikimedia.org/wiki/File:Installation_of_the_Sun_Goddess_(Amaterasu)_c1870_after_Kawanabe_Kyosai.jpg

[13] https://commons.wikimedia.org/wiki/File:Origin_of_the_Cave_Door_Dance_(Amaterasu)_by_Shunsai_Toshimasa_1889.jpg

[14] Douglas Perkins, CC BY 4.0 <https://creativecommons.org/licenses/by/4.0>, via Wikimedia Commons: https://commons.wikimedia.org/wiki/File:Ise_Jingu_02.jpg

[15] SLIMHANNYA, CC BY-SA 4.0 <https://creativecommons.org/licenses/by-sa/4.0>, via Wikimedia Commons: https://commons.wikimedia.org/wiki/File:Daisho_Uesugi_clan_2.jpg

[16] https://commons.wikimedia.org/wiki/File:Samurai-in-Armour-by-Kusakabe-Kimbei.png

[17] https://commons.wikimedia.org/wiki/File:Miyamoto-Musashi-Fights-Sasaki-Kojiro-at-Ganryujima-Ukiyo-e.png

[18] https://commons.wikimedia.org/wiki/File:Kanadehon-Chushingura-Stage-3-Utagawa-Kuniteru.png

[19] https://commons.wikimedia.org/wiki/File:Sengakuji_Ronin_Graves.jpg

[20] https://commons.wikimedia.org/wiki/File:Taketori_Monogatari_2.jpg

[21] ★Kumiko★ from Tokyo, Japan, CC BY-SA 2.0 <https://creativecommons.org/licenses/by-sa/2.0>, via Wikimedia Commons: https://commons.wikimedia.org/wiki/File:%E4%B8%83%E5%A4%95_(19545533256).jpg

[22] https://commons.wikimedia.org/wiki/File:Chikanobu_The_Boatman.jpg#filehistory

[23] https://commons.wikimedia.org/wiki/File:Dojoji_engi_emaki_-_p4.png

[24] https://commons.wikimedia.org/wiki/File:MasayoshiTofu-Kozo.jpg

[25] https://commons.wikimedia.org/wiki/File:Yoshitoshi_Driving_away_the_Demons.jpg

[26] https://commons.wikimedia.org/wiki/File:Hokusai_Sangoku_Yoko-den.jpg

[27] Miyuki Meinaka, CC BY-SA 4.0 <https://creativecommons.org/licenses/by-sa/4.0>, via Wikimedia Commons: https://commons.wikimedia.org/wiki/File:Splited_Sessho-Seki.jpg

[28] https://commons.wikimedia.org/wiki/File:Hokusai_tea-kettle_raccoon.jpg

[29] https://commons.wikimedia.org/wiki/File:Oni.jpg

[30] https://commons.wikimedia.org/wiki/File:Parelduikers_Pearl_divers.jpg

[31] https://commons.wikimedia.org/wiki/File:Jinjyoshogakukokugotokuhon-v3-p040.jpg

[32] https://commons.wikimedia.org/wiki/File:Matsuki_Heikichi(1899)-Urashima-p12.jpg

[33] https://commons.wikimedia.org/wiki/File:Matsuki_Heikichi(1899)-Urashima-p03.jpg

[34] https://commons.wikimedia.org/wiki/File:Kyoka_Hyaku-Monogatari_Kappa.jpg

[35] https://commons.wikimedia.org/wiki/File:Suushi_Yama-uba.jpg

[36] https://commons.wikimedia.org/wiki/File:YOSOJI%27S_CAMELLIA_TREE.jpg

[37] https://commons.wikimedia.org/wiki/File:Kosa_Yamato_Takeru_and_monster_fish.jpg

[38] *https://commons.wikimedia.org/wiki/File:Yamato-Takeru-with-Sword-Kusanagi-no-Tsurugi-by-Ogata-Gekko.png*

[39] *Motokoka, CC BY-SA 4.0 <https://creativecommons.org/licenses/by-sa/4.0>, via Wikimedia Commons: https://commons.wikimedia.org/wiki/File:Tengu_Masks,_Awashima_jinja_shrine_2.jpg*

[40] *https://commons.wikimedia.org/wiki/File:Yoshitsune_Training_with_the_Tengu_Sojobo_LACMA_M.81.31.530a-c_(cropped).jpg*

[41] *https://commons.wikimedia.org/wiki/File:Kuniyoshi_The_Ghost_in_the_Lantern.jpg*

[42] *https://commons.wikimedia.org/wiki/File:Yoshitoshi_Botan_Doro.jpg*

[43] *https://commons.wikimedia.org/wiki/File:Kabuki_actors_dressed_as_samurai_in_1880.jpg*

[44] *https://commons.wikimedia.org/wiki/File:Japanese_buddhist_monk_hat_by_Arashiyama_cut.jpg*

[45] *Naokijp, CC BY-SA 4.0 <https://creativecommons.org/licenses/by-sa/4.0>, via Wikimedia Commons: https://commons.wikimedia.org/wiki/File:Bandai-ji,_Jizo_Statue_001.jpg*

[46] *https://commons.wikimedia.org/wiki/File:Yoshitoshi_-_100_Aspects_of_the_Moon_-_97.jpg*

[47] *Luka Peternel, CC BY-SA 4.0 <https://creativecommons.org/licenses/by-sa/4.0>, via Wikimedia Commons: https://commons.wikimedia.org/wiki/File:Yoshino-yama-hills-cherry-blossom-2018-Luka-Peternel.jpg*

[48] *https://commons.wikimedia.org/wiki/File:Fan_of_Japanese_Cypress_ITUKUSHIMA_shrine.JPG*

Printed in Great Britain
by Amazon

47837319R00069